FIRST DRAFTS OF KOREA: THE U.S. MEDIA AND PERCEPTIONS OF THE LAST COLD WAR FRONTIER

Edited by
Donald A. L. Macintyre, Daniel C.
Sneider, and Gi-Wook Shin

SHORENSTEIN
APARC
STANFORD

THE WALTER H. SHORENSTEIN
ASIA-PACIFIC RESEARCH CENTER

THE WALTER H. SHORENSTEIN ASIA-PACIFIC RESEARCH CENTER (Shorenstein APARC) is a unique Stanford University institution focused on the interdisciplinary study of contemporary Asia. Shorenstein APARC's mission is to produce and publish outstanding interdisciplinary, Asia-Pacific–focused research; to educate students, scholars, and corporate and governmental affiliates; to promote constructive interaction to influence U.S. policy toward the Asia-Pacific; and to guide Asian nations on key issues of societal transition, development, U.S.-Asia relations, and regional cooperation.

The Walter H. Shorenstein Asia-Pacific Research Center
Freeman Spogli Institute for International Studies
Stanford University
Encina Hall
Stanford, CA 94305-6055
tel. 650-723-9741
fax 650-723-6530
http://APARC.stanford.edu

First Drafts of Korea: The U.S. Media and Perceptions of the Last Cold War Frontier may be ordered from:
The Brookings Institution
c/o DFS, P.O. Box 50370, Baltimore, MD, USA
tel. 1-800-537-5487 or 410-516-6956
fax 410-516-6998
http://www.brookings.edu/press

First printing, 2009.
13-digit ISBN 978-1-931368-15-5

FIRST DRAFTS
OF KOREA:
THE U.S. MEDIA
AND PERCEPTIONS
OF THE LAST COLD
WAR FRONTIER

SHORENSTEIN
APARC
STANFORD

THE WALTER H. SHORENSTEIN
ASIA-PACIFIC RESEARCH CENTER

CONTENTS

ACKNOWLEDGMENTS

The papers collected in this volume were first presented at a conference of the same name, held in July 2007 at the Walter H. Shorenstein Asia-Pacific Research Center at Stanford University. We are grateful to Shorenstein APARC for providing financial and staff support for this successful and thought-provoking gathering. Discussion among the distinguished conference participants was lively and wide-ranging, and we hope that this volume conveys that energy. Many thanks to the contributors—Kristin C. Burke, Caroline Gluck, Martin Fackler, Anna Fifield, Chris Nelson, B. R. Myers, David E. Sanger, Karl Schoenberger, Barbara Slavin, David Straub, and Doug Struck—each of whom carved time out of demanding schedules to revise their work for the publication.

For its generous financial support of the conference, we thank the Pantech Fund for Korean Studies. We also thank, as ever, Walter H. Shorenstein for his steadfast interest in and support of this and other activities at the research center that bears his name. Shorenstein APARC staff, too, were crucial to the entire process—Heather Ahn organized the conference and handled complex logistics, while Victoria Tomkinson edited and designed the resulting volume. Fayre Makeig provided able and unflinching copyediting.

We hope that the publication of this volume, with its deliberate mix of academic scholarship and journalistic storytelling, will assist scholars, policymakers, and the general public in understanding how news coverage decisions and the stories that followed have shaped the way Americans conceptualize both Koreas, the alliance between the United States and the Republic of Korea (ROK), and the North Korean nuclear crises.

—Donald A. L. Macintyre, Daniel C. Sneider, and Gi-Wook Shin
June 2009

A foreign reporter takes a picture of a South Korean coast guard during a press tour. *Credit:* Stringer Korea/Reuters.

INTRODUCTION

Donald A. L. Macintyre, Daniel C. Sneider, and Gi-Wook Shin

Few countries in the world rival the Republic of Korea (ROK, or South Korea) in its strategic importance to U.S. foreign policy. For more than half a century, tens of thousands of American troops, including major units of the U.S. Army and Air Force, have been stationed in South Korea—the front line of the United States' guarantee to defend that nation. South Korea is considered essential to the defense of Japan, an ally that is the linchpin of American interests in East Asia. Meanwhile, the Democratic People's Republic of Korea (DPRK, or North Korea), now armed with nuclear weapons, has consistently topped the list of potential security threats to the United States.

South Korea's emergence as a prosperous and dynamic market-based democracy has added another dimension to its weight in American strategic calculations. Its economy is the thirteenth largest in the world, almost equal in size to that of India and larger than that of Mexico. South Korean corporations are leaders in the high-technology sector, and their products join those of Japan and Germany as prized consumer goods. South Korea ranks among the top trading partners of the United States, and South Koreans constitute one of the largest groups of international students on American college campuses.

Despite its importance to U.S. interests, however, South Korea has rarely, and only episodically, registered on Americans' radar screen. U.S. involvement in Korea at the close of World War II was almost accidental, with little of the planning given to the postwar occupation of Japan. American troops withdrew from Korea by 1948, and had Kim Il-sung not launched his ill-advised invasion of the south in 1950—premised on the belief that the United States would not intervene—the U.S. commitment to Korea would likely have been limited. Even after the Korean War, though U.S. troops remained, American interest in the peninsula quickly waned.

In subsequent years, South Korea has been underrepresented by the U.S. media. Other allies such as the United Kingdom and Japan attract four and six times the amount of media attention, respectively. And although its economic importance to the United States is comparable to that of Russia, Israel, and France, all three receive significantly more news coverage than the ROK. Instead, South Korea's coverage is comparable to that of Switzerland, Argentina, and Indonesia, each of which is less important to the United States from an economic and security perspective. As Daniel C. Sneider points out in chapter 3 of this book, "American policymakers have historically given very little thought to Korea itself . . . [and the] U.S. media have tended to follow this same pattern."

This book examines the previously unexplored gap between American perceptions of South Korea and the nation's strategic importance. In particular, the authors look at how the American mass media have helped shape those perceptions and thus affected foreign policy and international relations. True, cultural influences have likewise begun to influence mutual perception. In recent years, South Korean products such as Samsung cell phones and Hyundai cars have become popular among American consumers. South Korean students still flock to U.S. higher education institutions and America's Korean American population continues to grow. Nevertheless, Americans have tended to view both North and South Korea through the eyes of the media, not firsthand.

How, then, have the American media covered the Koreas? What issues dominate the agenda of American reporters and editors? What has the tone of the coverage been like? How have the scale and scope of U.S. media coverage of the Korean Peninsula stacked up against reporting on other parts of the world? How has coverage of North Korea compared with that of South Korea? And how have these trends evolved over time?

To answer these important questions, Professor Gi-Wook Shin and his research team at Stanford University's Walter H. Shorenstein Asia-Pacific Research Center carried out a detailed study, the first of its kind, of American media coverage of the Korean Peninsula. The study gathered data that underpin a long-term quantitative analysis of the coverage that three major American newspapers—the *New York Times,* the *Wall Street Journal,* and the *Washington Post*—accorded to the peninsula between 1992 and 2003. *First Drafts of Korea* focuses specifically on the amount and tone of American coverage of the Koreas during this period. A second book, which explores the broader theme of how the media in *both* South Korea and the United States have influenced U.S.-ROK relations, is currently being prepared for publication.[1]

Shin's research team found new evidence—detailed in chapter 1—of several significant trends in American coverage of the Koreas. These are generally consistent with conventional expectations but are, in some cases, counterintuitive. First, the study data clearly indicate that coverage of Korean affairs is driven even more heavily by the dynamics of "hot-spot" journalism than are other major stories. As Shin and his coauthor, Kristin C. Burke, point out, "all three newspapers exhibit significant 'spikes' in coverage around 1994, 1997, and 2002–2003. These periods of relatively high coverage correspond to major crises and their fallout—the first North Korean nuclear crisis, the Asian financial crisis, and the second North Korean nuclear crisis, respectively."

Such hot-spot journalism also accounted for an earlier spike, around the time of the democratic uprising against authoritarian rule in 1987. During this period, the media covered some events but focused in particular on anti-American sentiments in South Korea. After this spike, however, coverage of ongoing key issues—such as democratization and economic transformation—dropped off dramatically and has seldom been revived.

Second, the Shin research team study examined the U.S. media's tone in coverage of South Korea, whether in news articles or in editorial and opinion pages. The study concluded that the overall tone is somewhat negative—in part because of the media focus on crises—and particularly when it comes to news stories. A negative slant is even more discernible in coverage of North Korea, which tends to focus on the country's nuclear weapons program and on issues such as human rights violations and mass famine. This finding confirms the public perception that the media often gravitates toward negative stories on the basis that bad news sells.

The study's third conclusion is that American media coverage of the Korean Peninsula is persistently focused on security issues in general, and on those related to North Korea in particular. This is more true for some papers than for others. The *Washington Post*, for example, devoted far more ink to security issues than did the *New York Times* and the *Wall Street Journal*, suggesting that the agenda of Washington policymakers drives the coverage of that influential daily. Moreover, the reporting for stories on security issues originated almost as frequently from Washington as from Seoul or the region; this was the case even for stories about North Korea's nuclear program, where Washington-based reporters originated more than half the coverage.

While these broad research results may come as no surprise, the finding that U.S. media coverage of South Korea tends to downplay the U.S.-ROK security alliance, despite the massive presence of American troops there, is unexpected.[2] Instead, American journalists focus on domestic events in South Korea—ranging from politics to culture—and also, to an important extent, on the economy, including trade relations with the United States. As Shin and Burke write, "the ROK, as a major trading partner, has importance to the United States beyond the security alliance; indeed, the alliance is not the primary basis for American interest in the country." It is little wonder, then, that many Americans view South Korea as synonymous with electronics and cars, and have only vague and static notions of the country's military importance to the United States.

In July 2007 key results of the Shin research team's macro-level, data-driven study were presented to a gathering of prominent Western journalists, many of whom had actively covered the Korean Peninsula since the 1980s, together with former and current U.S. officials deeply involved in U.S. public diplomacy toward the region. The group convened at Stanford University to reflect on the study and to share their personal experiences in creating the "first drafts of Korea." The journalists were grouped into three categories, by area of focus:

- South Korea, including its democratization, the rise of anti-Americanism and Korean nationalism, and the nation's emergence as an economic powerhouse

- North Korea (with extensive experience in directly reporting from the North)
- The North Korean nuclear crisis (with reporting done largely out of Washington)

Journalists in all three groups were asked to reflect on their personal experiences and answer several basic questions: What did they cover and what drove their coverage decisions? How much did the U.S. government set the agenda for their coverage? What other factors determined the level of U.S. interest in Korea? Finally, what were the chief obstacles to providing balanced coverage?

The journalist accounts gathered in this book illustrate, often in very personal detail, the challenges of covering Korea. They confirm the problem of hot-spot journalism and the difficulty of maintaining sustained coverage of complex issues, such as democratic transformation, once the media crisis spotlight had moved elsewhere. "Hot spots are not all bad," observes Karl Schoenberger, who covered the Koreas for the *Los Angeles Times* beginning in the late 1980s. They can bring international attention to an important event, as was the case with South Korea's democratic uprising in 1986–1988. Unfortunately, as he points out in chapter 2, "most of the foreign journalists packed up and left for better hunting grounds not long after the closing ceremony of the Seoul Olympic Games, leaving audiences to guess what happened to the progress of a nascent democracy."

In chapter 3, Daniel C. Sneider reflects on his experiences covering Korea for the *Christian Science Monitor* during the 1980s. He considers how South Korea's democratic transformation, including the rise of anti-Americanism that accompanied it, became the dominant story that he and his colleagues told at the time. That coverage peaked between 1987 and 1988, almost entirely due to the dramatic political story that was unfolding. Security issues related to the United States were a minor theme, Sneider writes, marking a rare moment when "Koreans were the main actors, with Americans playing an important but secondary role."

This focus on Koreans themselves was fleeting and almost never repeated except at long interludes. Even during spikes of coverage, such as the one brought about by the second nuclear crisis of 2002–2003, the Koreas remained a relatively minor story. In chapter 11, David E. Sanger, the chief Washington correspondent for the *New York Times*, points out a particular irony he noted in the course of covering the North Korean nuclear issue. In 2002, while the media were focused on allegations that Iraq was harboring weapons of mass destruction, they paid very little attention to North Korea's open move toward developing nuclear weapons. Sanger identifies the government's power to set the news agenda as the underlying reason for this blind spot. "Precisely because the president wanted to focus American attention elsewhere," Sanger remarks, "journalists found it extremely difficult to spark much interest in the strategic implications of a North Korea with eight or more weapons."

Barbara Slavin, who covered the nuclear crisis for more than a decade for *USA Today*, offers similar glimpses of administration officials' efforts to shape and influence stories about North Korea's nuclear aspirations. In chapter 10 she too notes how, with the Iraq war buildup in full swing, Bush administration officials "refused to label the situation a crisis, and my editors seemed to agree." North Korea's reluctance to grant U.S. reporters access to cover the situation added another layer of difficulty.

In chapter 13, Chris Nelson is sharply critical of the media's failure to get beyond official pronouncements in its coverage of the Korean Peninsula in general and the North Korean nuclear crisis in particular. The editor of *The Nelson Report*, the authoritative newsletter on Asia policy, he presents the results of a survey of policymakers focused on the peninsula, who detailed their use of American media and other sources of information to influence public debate. It is a mixed and not entirely encouraging picture; Nelson points to the "vast room for improvement" in the performance of both U.S. and South Korean news editors and reporters.

The efforts of American officials to shape coverage pales in comparison with the North Korean regime's crude attempts to control the depiction of their country in the Western media. Three chapters in the book—chapter 6, by Donald A. L. Macintyre, *Time* magazine's former Seoul bureau chief; chapter 7, by Anna Fifield of the *Financial Times*; and chapter 9, by Caroline Gluck, formerly of the BBC—provide detailed and fascinating accounts of their multiple but often frustrating visits to the so-called Hermit Kingdom. Gluck, for example, recalls that her travel into North Korea in the early 2000s, "like all trips to the North, was carefully choreographed." Even when there was what seemed to be a spontaneous encounter with an ordinary North Korean, the reporter could never be sure if it was truly unplanned. "Nothing is quite as it seems in North Korea," she concludes.

To be sure, obtaining reliable sources of information about North Korea remains a constant challenge. "I know of no Western journalists who have sources in North Korea in the usual sense of the word," writes Macintyre. North Korean defectors whom he sought out provided a wealth of information on everyday life, as well as topics such as the spread of the underground economy. At times, however, they could be less than reliable, particularly on nuclear and security questions. In the end, Macintyre asserts that coverage of North Korea was perpetually subject to the circumscribed and shifting attentions of editors and others back home. "Unless events are likely to have a direct impact on the United States," he states, "there is often little interest."

Financial Times correspondent Fifield, who tried to reach beyond the nuclear issue to write about economic and social changes in North Korea, observes that "interest in North Korea tends to fade quickly—the July 2006 missile tests were in the news for only a few days, soon bumped by the Israeli-Lebanese conflict. Indeed, interest in the tests fizzled almost as quickly as the devices tested."

Journalists—especially foreign correspondents—are constantly vexed by the scant opportunities to place stories in their wider context. Limitations of space and attention often mean that events are treated as discrete entities, without reference to ongoing trends or their historical precedents. In chapter 8, B. R. Myers, a South Korea–based contributing editor for *The Atlantic*, argues that the Western media have failed to provide just such a context for writing about North Korea. "Western journalists," he writes, "regard North Korea's ideology and official culture as interference," preferring to focus instead on "Kim Jong-il's hairstyle and his taste in cognac." In chapter 4, Doug Struck echoes this sentiment. As the Tokyo-based correspondent for the *Washington Post* from 1999 to 2003, Struck covered a period that included momentous events in Korean history—from the first North Korea–South Korea summit meeting in 2000 to the upsurge in anti-Americanism that led Roh Moo-hyun to victory in the 2002 presidential election. In Struck's view, the published stories about these developments "offered up only a thin slice of the fuller explanation for those events." When it came to anti-Americanism, "the reporting was not wrong, but it failed to encompass enough of the emotional mix of the time. . . . we did not connect all the dots."

David Straub, who served in the U.S. Embassy in Seoul from 1993 to 2003, shares Struck's opinion. "The U.S. media," Straub notes in chapter 12, "were unable . . . to present a complete picture to readers and viewers, due largely to the complexity of the situation and the inherent limitations of reporting on foreign affairs for a general American audience." Straub also focuses sharply on how the shortcomings of the Korean media constrained U.S. diplomats' ability to shape perceptions of the United States and its foreign policy. South Korean journalists and editors, he notes, had locked themselves into a negative story line about the United States: "Items that fit into the 'Ugly American' story line were covered; those that did not, were not highlighted."

No treatment of journalism or foreign coverage would be complete without a lament, sounded by many contributors to this book, about shrinking coverage as a result of financial cutbacks. Historically, the Tokyo bureaus of major newspapers, television networks, and other news agencies, as well as the offices of wire services and freelance contributors based in Seoul, took responsibility for covering and managing the coverage of South Korea. In the late 1980s, however, South Korea's emergence as an economic power prompted some newspapers, including the *Wall Street Journal*, to open full-fledged bureaus in Seoul. In recent years, other newspapers and magazines, such as the *Los Angeles Times* and *Time* magazine, followed suit. But as *New York Times* correspondent Martin Fackler reports in chapter 5 of this volume, financial pressures have since forced many Western media outlets to shutter not only their Seoul bureaus, but also to reduce—if not close—their Tokyo operations. Today, with the exception of three newspapers (the *Wall Street Journal*, the *Financial Times*, and the *International Herald Tribune*), *BusinessWeek* magazine, and the wire services, the job of covering the Koreas is done in Tokyo, Beijing, or U.S. cities. As Fackler puts it, these developments reflect a shift in focus as well as finances. "Even the handful of newspapers, including the *New York Times*, that have maintained their overall number of overseas bureaus have been forced to shift resources out of Northeast Asia to offset the enormous costs of covering the war in Iraq," he observes. Moreover, the "news hole"—the amount of actual space available for stories in newspapers such as the *New York Times* and the *Wall Street Journal*—has shrunk due to financial pressures. As Fareed Zakaria (editor of Newsweek International) has written, the United States has globalized the world but it has not globalized the perspectives of its own people—a shortcoming borne out all too clearly in U.S. press coverage of Korean affairs.

First Drafts of Korea offers a unique and sweeping view of American media coverage of the Korean Peninsula, its processes and pitfalls, and its impact on policymaking. Grounded in the quantitative and qualitative data analysis of Gi-Wook Shin and his colleagues, the book is complemented by the firsthand accounts of men and women who have worked to understand this vital part of the world. A complex and shifting portrait emerges, as befits a nation that is itself evolving and growing in global importance.

Notes

[1] Gi-Wook Shin, *One Alliance, Two Lenses: U.S.-Korea Relations in a New Era* (Stanford, CA: Stanford University Press, 2009).

[2] In contrast, security is a major subject in Korean press coverage of U.S. and U.S.-ROK relations. Unlike Americans, many South Koreans are reminded of the alliance on a daily basis, confronted as they are by U.S. troops in their country. See Shin, *One Alliance, Two Lenses.*

OVERVIEW AND TRENDS

Chun Yung-woo, South Korea's chief negotiator for the Six-Party Talks in 2007, addresses journalists. *Credit:* Reuters/Claro Cortes.

THE TWO KOREAS
IN THE AMERICAN NEWS, 1992–2004

Gi-Wook Shin and Kristin C. Burke

This chapter offers an overview of U.S. press coverage of the two Koreas from July 1992 to January 2004. We seek to describe how the U.S. media covered the Republic of Korea (ROK, or South Korea) and the Democratic People's Republic of Korea (DPRK, or North Korea) and to examine these nations' relevance to various U.S. interests. This survey addresses a number of questions, such as: In American newspapers' coverage of the Korean Peninsula, is the ROK or DPRK covered more? What types of issues attract U.S. interest? More specifically, which garner more coverage—security interests or economic interests? Which issues are more prominent in ROK coverage than in DPRK coverage, and vice versa? For example, how does the attention devoted to America's ostensibly troubled alliance with the ROK (during the latter years of the study period) compare with that focused on the DPRK's nuclear weapons development? And has the American media's portrayal of the two Koreas changed over time? If so, were the changes event-specific or part of a trend?

To answer these questions, we analyze two dimensions of U.S. media coverage of the two Koreas: *news attention* and *news tone*. We then examine articles by two criteria: first, their *focus*, which refers to the country or bilateral relationship that they cover (such as the ROK or U.S.-ROK relations), and, second, their *issue*, which refers to the major topic area (such as security, economics, or domestic politics). Where appropriate, we also mention the news *subject*, which refers to a more specific topic or subject matter, such as North Korean weapons of mass destruction (WMD) or South Korean labor relations.

The period examined in this chapter encompasses the end of the Cold War, South Korean democratization, the beginnings of inter-Korean rapprochement, two nuclear crises, and the U.S. war on terror, and thus offers a good window through which to examine American press coverage of the two Koreas across changing contexts. South Korean democratization and the end of the Cold War in particular fostered an environment that led South Koreans to rethink their place in the region and the world, and to question conventional views of their nation's relations with the United States and North Korea. During the 1992–2004 period we study here, the United States dealt with two nuclear stand-offs with the North, the latter of which occurred in the post-9/11 environment. As North Korean issues are widely perceived to be a critical factor in the changing U.S.-ROK relationship, this period presents a fascinating opportunity to examine that connection.

For this study, we selected three U.S. newspapers: the *New York Times*, the *Washington Post*, and the *Wall Street Journal*.[1] As the self-proclaimed "paper of record," the *Times* is the most influential of the three, often setting the agenda of other media outlets in the United States, especially in the domain of foreign affairs. The *Post* is another authoritative source in foreign affairs coverage. In addition to the *Times* and the *Post*, we have elected to include the *Wall Street Journal*. By including the *Journal*, a leading conservative newspaper, in our study, we are able to represent a wider spectrum of ideological perspectives, as the other two newspapers are broadly believed to have slightly liberal leanings. The *Journal* is the most influential news source in the financial sector and thus can capture economic and trade-related topics—both important elements of U.S.-ROK relations.

The data set examined in this chapter consists of a total of 5,053 articles published in the three dailies between July 1992 and January 2004.[2] Of these, 2,102 were published in the *New York Times*, 1,217 in the *Washington Post*, and 1,734 in the *Wall Street Journal*. A vast majority of stories were original articles (88.6 percent), while the remainder were newswire stories fed by the Associated Press (AP) or Reuters. In relative terms, the *Times* relied most heavily on newswire services, although its original articles (79.4 percent) still predominated.

Among those articles in the data set with datelines that identify location, 52.9 percent were reported from Seoul and 13.1 percent from Washington, D.C. Only 1.5 percent of articles were reported from Pyongyang (North Korea). The *Wall Street Journal* had the most articles reported from Seoul (69.8 percent). Articles on U.S.-DPRK relations, especially on North Korea's WMD program, were most frequently covered from Washington, D.C.

News stories were the most represented article type in American news about Korea, composing just over 73 percent of the sample. Special features were the second most represented, at approximately 12 percent of the sample, and editorials constituted just over 3 percent of the entire U.S. news sample. The *New York Times* published many more Korea-related special features than either of the other newspapers, both in absolute and proportional terms. The *Washington Post* carried many more regular and guest columns on Korea than the other newspapers.

The data contain what we categorized as *descriptive* and *evaluative* articles. Descriptive articles focus on providing factual information, whereas evaluative ones primarily contain the author's interpretation and assessment of factual information and/or predictions regarding future developments. Nearly half (48.49 percent) of the sample's articles were primarily descriptive, almost one-fourth (22.71 percent) contained primarily evaluative content, and slightly more than one-fourth (26.49 percent) contained both descriptive and evaluative content.

The Two Koreas in U.S. News

We begin our examination of U.S. news coverage of the Korean Peninsula by comparing the amount of attention the three newspapers gave to South Korea and North Korea between July 1992 and January 2004. The U.S. news media distributes its attention across a wide range of Korea-related issues and subjects, largely according to how important they seem to U.S. interests. Tracking the volume of U.S. media attention paid to each topic—which in turn affects the level of attention paid by the American public—can approximate how the American public and American policymakers perceive and prioritize what is happening on the Korean Peninsula. Measuring media attention on the ROK versus the DPRK is also important, as the relative visibility of each nation and its predominating issues may frame how the American public otherwise perceives the Korean Peninsula.

News Focus[3]

In U.S. coverage of the Korean Peninsula during the study period, news about the ROK (tagged as "ROK" plus "U.S.-ROK relations" in the data set) received more coverage than news about the DPRK (tagged as "DPRK" plus "U.S.-DPRK relations"). When pooled across newspapers, approximately 46.3 percent of the articles in the sample featured news about the ROK and U.S.-ROK relations, while 38.6 percent of articles featured DPRK-related news. Articles on inter-Korean relations accounted for 8.4 percent of the U.S. news sample (see table 1.1).

Table 1.1 Focus of articles in three U.S. newspapers (July 1992–January 2004)

Focus	New York Times	Washington Post	Wall Street Journal	All
All ROK	43.2%	20.1%	68.6%	46.3%
	908	246	1,190	2,344
ROK	35.3%	12.2%	57.6%	37.4%
	742	149	999	1,890
U.S.-ROK relations	7.9%	7.9%	11%	8.9%
	166	97	191	454
All DPRK	38%	61.7%	23.1%	38.6%
	801	752	402	1,955
DPRK	9.1%	15.6%	7.4%	10.1%
	193	190	129	512
U.S.-DPRK relations	28.9%	46.1%	15.7%	28.5%
	608	562	273	1,443
ROK-DPRK relations	10.8%	9.6%	4.6%	8.4%
	229	117	80	426
Total (%)	100	100	100	100
Total (number)	2,102	1,217	1,734	5,053

It is interesting to note that articles about the ROK are far more prevalent than articles about U.S.-ROK relations—37.4 percent versus 8.9 percent of the total sample. This dynamic is most pronounced in the case of the *Wall Street Journal*, which accorded 57.6 percent of its Korean Peninsula coverage to the ROK and only 11 percent to U.S.-ROK relations. This imbalance likely reflects the financial newspaper's greater interest in and coverage of the ROK's vibrant economy.[4] The data demonstrate that the ROK is of greater interest to the U.S. public than the U.S.-ROK alliance.

Conversely, the three U.S. newspapers in this study all published more articles about the U.S.-DPRK relationship (28.5 percent) than about the DPRK itself (10.1 percent). Certainly—and as the foreign correspondents featured in this volume testify—part of this discrepancy is due to the barriers that the North Korean regime imposes on the flow of information. Pyongyang allows entry to very few journalists and circumscribes the activities of those who are admitted. As Donald A. L. Macintyre (chapter 6), Anna Fifield (chapter 7), and Caroline Gluck (chapter 9), and Barbara Slavin (chapter 10) attest, journalists' ability to write well-researched and well-sourced stories about the DPRK has been severely constrained. In keeping with these limitations, it is not surprising that only forty-six articles from our entire data set were reported from Pyongyang. Beyond information restrictions, the dominance of U.S.-DPRK news over DPRK news suggests something about American perceptions of North Korea and its relative importance. The country seems to attract significant American media attention only when its behavior—such as its pursuit of nuclear weapons—leads Americans to believe that it is a security problem *requiring* U.S. attention and/or intervention. As Macintyre points out in chapter 6, unless events in North Korea have a direct impact on the United States and its interests, the country is often a hard sell to newspaper editors. Indeed, our data show that DPRK-related issues did not appear much in the U.S. news until the story of the first nuclear crisis broke in 1993.

When examined by article type, the ROK and the U.S.-ROK relationship both yielded a relatively high percentage of special features (both approximately 16 percent), a primarily descriptive article type. The DPRK and the U.S.-DPRK relationship, by contrast, were associated with lower rates of coverage through special features (5.3 percent and 6.9 percent, respectively). It may well be that more special features focus on ROK-related topics because this country is perceived to be generally more dynamic and more accessible than the DPRK.

The U.S.-DPRK relationship, however, yielded the greatest amount of evaluative analysis and was the subject of a very high proportion of the total number of regular columns and guest columns—49 of 60 and 66 of 90, respectively. Stories about the U.S.-DPRK relationship also accounted for more than half of the total number of unsigned editorials and letters in the U.S. news sample (94 out of 174). This finding suggests that this relationship presents a significant policy challenge. While other focus categories of our study may be associated with newsworthy events covered in a primarily descriptive fashion, the U.S.-DPRK relationship and security concerns about the DPRK spark intense debate over policy options.

One of the most interesting inter-newspaper differences that emerges from this data is that the *Washington Post* devoted the majority of its Korean Peninsula coverage to the DPRK and U.S.-DPRK relations (61.7 percent), while the *Wall Street Journal* devoted most of its coverage to the ROK and U.S.-ROK relations (68.6 percent). This contrast is likely due to several factors, including the *Washington Post*'s penchant for security and foreign policy news—as befits its location inside the Washington Beltway—and the *Journal*'s attraction to the ROK's dynamic economy as opposed to the DPRK's stagnant and faltering one.

Issues Addressed[5]

In our assessment of U.S. news about the entire Korean Peninsula (see table 1.2), we found that security matters received the most prominent attention (39.1 percent), followed closely by economic issues (34.5 percent). Domestic politics (7.5 percent),[6] general diplomatic matters (6.1 percent), and humanitarian and human rights issues (5.8 percent) all received significantly less attention. This finding suggests that in the eyes of the U.S. media, *security and economics are the most important issues on the Korean Peninsula.* In terms of specific subject matter, as shown in table 1.3, North Korea's WMD constituted the single most prominent topic in U.S. news coverage of the entire peninsula. The high degree of focus on this issue—and general security concerns related to the DPRK—frames American perceptions of the Korean Peninsula and plausibly channels the attention of America's policymakers away from other topics related to the two Koreas, such as the rapid change and development in South Korea.

The security/military issue was strongly associated with evaluative articles, including regular and guest columns, unsigned editorials, and letters. The economy/trade issue, by contrast, was strongly associated with descriptive articles, most notably special features. Once again, this finding is consistent with our expectations, as a security issue tends to spur intense debate over the nature of the threat and policy options, whereas economic issues—less often contentious—are generally covered more descriptively.

As in other dimensions of our analysis, the three newspapers differed in the relative attention they paid to each of these issues, as shown in table 1.2. As expected, *Journal* articles on the Korean Peninsula primarily focused on economic issues (61.5 percent), while security was the second most frequently reported topic (23.8 percent). In contrast, security issues dominated coverage in the *Times* (39.5 percent) and, to an even greater extent, the *Post* (60.3 percent). These newspapers devoted 27.7 percent and 7.8 percent of their coverage, respectively, to economic matters.

As table 1.2 shows, evaluating the news coverage of the ROK and DPRK separately provides a more precise picture than viewing them in aggregate. Within these newspapers' coverage of the ROK, only 8.8 percent of stories were devoted to security issues, while a substantial 65 percent focused on economic issues. Indeed, all three newspapers accorded the majority of their ROK news coverage to economic issues, though in varying degrees. The time period of our sample, 1992–2004, covers years of rapid economic development as well as precipitous economic crisis; this high proportion of economic coverage is therefore in keeping with events. Indeed, despite recent headlines during the latter years of this study announcing strains in the alliance between the United States and the ROK, American interest in South Korea's economy and trade relations with the United States remains strong. At the time of this writing, this interest is being expressed most conspicuously through pursuit of the Korea-U.S. Free Trade Agreement (KORUS FTA), which has become a strategic initiative as U.S. policy elites declare that the relationship has been artificially focused on security for too long.[7] In this vein, it is interesting to note that topics related to the U.S.-ROK or ROK-DPRK alliances do not occupy a central position in U.S. newspaper coverage of the ROK. Meanwhile, these issues have spurred serious policy differences in recent years and continue to occupy government leaders in all the nations concerned.

For the DPRK, in contrast, an overwhelming 74.3 percent of U.S. newspaper coverage focused on security matters, while only 5.5 percent pertained to economic issues. Even the *Wall Street Journal* deviated only negligibly from the other two newspapers in this respect, with over 70 percent of its DPRK coverage clustering around security issues. This established tendency in coverage suggests that the DPRK does not receive much media attention unless it poses a security problem for the United States.

Human rights and humanitarian topics were the second most prominent issues in DPRK news, capturing 10.8 percent and 9.8 percent of related coverage in the *New York Times* and the *Washington Post,* respectively. This reflects bipartisan American concern over the human rights situation in North Korea—concern expressed most tangibly through the U.S. House of Representatives' and the Senate's unanimous passage of the North Korean Human Rights Act of 2004, as well as the prevalence of defector accounts in reports on North Korea.[8]

Specific Subjects

The relative prominence of security and human rights issues was reflected in our analysis of the specific subjects addressed. As table 1.3 shows, North Korea's WMD programs constituted the single most prominent topic within U.S. news coverage of the Korean Peninsula, commanding just under one-third of all coverage (29.68 percent). The *Washington Post* accorded nearly half (49.54 percent) of its peninsular coverage to the WMD story, more than the other two papers. Across the three papers, the country's pursuit of WMD captured 64.9 percent of all coverage of the DRPK. The second most popular DPRK-related subject was human rights, at 9.15 percent. The U.S.-DPRK military conflict ranked third (5.46 percent), general diplomacy fourth (4.58 percent), and North

Korean politics fifth (4.06 percent). No economic topics ranked in the five most prevalent DPRK subjects covered by the three newspapers.

Table 1.2 Issues addressed by three U.S. newspapers (July 1992–January 2004)

Issue	New York Times (%)	Washington Post (%)	Wall Street Journal (%)	All (%)
All				
Security	39.5	60.3	23.8	39.1
Domestic politics	8.7	7.2	6.2	7.5
Economic issues	27.7	8.0	61.5	34.5
General diplomacy	7.7	8.1	2.8	6.1
Human rights issues	7.4	8.7	1.8	5.8
Others	9	8	4	7
Total	100%	100%	100%	100%
All ROK				
Security	9.9	20.3	5.5	8.8
Domestic politics	15.9	23.1	7.32	12.3
Economic issues	54.1	25.6	81.5	65
General diplomacy	3.3	6.9	1.4	2.7
Human rights issues	1.8	2.8	0.3	1.2
Others	25.0	21.3	4	10
Total	100%	100%	100%	100%
All DPRK				
Security	71.3	78.4	72.6	74.3
Domestic politics	3.5	3.4	5.47	3.8
Economic issues	4.8	2.5	12.4	5.5
General diplomacy	7.6	4.5	2.7	5.4
Human rights issues	10.5	9.7	5.2	9.1
Others	2	1	2	2
Total	100%	100%	100%	100%

Note: "All" = "All ROK" + "All DPRK" + ROK-DPRK relations; "All ROK" = ROK + U.S.-ROK relations; "All DPRK" = DPRK + U.S.-DPRK relations

In sharp contrast, economics and trade accounted for four of the five most prevalent subjects in U.S. coverage of the ROK, with the South Korean economy and industry receiving the most coverage at 40.55 percent, the Korean economic crisis receiving the second highest amount at 13.69 percent, and U.S.-ROK trade and "other economy" subjects ranking fourth and fifth, respectively. The only noneconomic subject that ranked among the top five was domestic politics. No security-related subjects made the top five. It makes sense that that the specific subject of domestic politics received more coverage than security, since general ROK news is more common than U.S.-ROK news. This trend may also reflect the relative stability of the U.S.-ROK alliance over most of the study years, even in the face of North Korean missile and nuclear weapons development.

Overall, the findings presented in table 1.3 show that DPRK coverage is more similar across the three newspapers than ROK coverage, apparently due to overwhelming concern over North Korea's pursuit of WMD as well as its human rights violations. By focusing on only two subjects, U.S. newspapers reinforce an image of North Korea as a threatening Communist regime.

Descriptive versus Evaluative Articles

We now examine the type and tone of newspaper articles written about the Korean Peninsula overall and the ROK and DPRK in particular. We rate each article's descriptive and evaluative elements on a 5-point scale ranging from –2 for "primarily negative" to 2 for "primarily positive," with 0 for mixed, ambiguous, or neutral.[9] We then compare the points given to each type and highlight instances where there are disparities between the two. When the evaluative articles on any one of our three categories (*focus, issue,* and *subject*) are more negative than the descriptive articles, this indicates that the newspaper's *assessment* of the topic is more negative than the topic itself. This is often true for contentious categories that carry strong implications beyond specific events. Sometimes a category's evaluative elements are more positive than its descriptive elements, however, indicating that a newspaper's assessment of events is less harsh than the events themselves may appear.

Evaluating article tone by focus category

As table 1.4 shows, the newspapers' coverage of every focus topic was almost all negative, across descriptive and evaluative elements. The average tone of descriptive Korean Peninsula news was –0.39, and the average tone of evaluative news was –0.44. U.S. news about the Korean Peninsula can therefore be described as somewhat negative, if 0 is considered the point of neutrality. Yet in light of the media's negativity bias—the assumption that bad news sells more papers than good news—this result does not necessarily indicate an unfavorable evaluation of the Korean Peninsula.

Table 1.3 Specific subjects addressed by three U.S. newspapers (July 1992–January 2004)

Subject	New York Times (%)	Washington Post (%)	Wall Street Journal (%)	All (%)
All				
North Korea's WMD (including nuclear, chemical/biological, and missile programs)	27.61	49.54	18.3	29.68
South Korean economy/industry (general)	16.48	0.5	36.43	19.56
Korean economic (financial) crisis	5.11	3.95	9.88	6.49
Human rights issues in North Korea	6.95	8.75	1.87	5.62
Other general diplomacy	6.9	7.06	2.69	5.48
ROK				
South Korean economy/industry (general)	36.31	2.53	51.36	40.55
Korean economic (financial) crisis	11.23	19.41	14.37	13.69
South Korean domestic politics (other than election)	12.14	14.35	5.36	8.88
South Korea-U.S. trade	3.32	3.38	9.44	6.47
Other economy	1.95	0	4.85	3.24
DPRK				
North Korea's WMD (including nuclear, chemical/biological, and missile programs)	59.8	69.66	65.99	64.9
Human rights issues in North Korea	10.63	9.66	5.29	9.15
U.S.-North Korea military conflict (unrelated to WMD issues)	7.55	5.1	2.02	5.46
Other general diplomacy	6.02	4.03	2.77	4.58
North Korean politics	3.71	3.76	5.29	4.06

Table 1.4 The average tone of descriptive and evaluative news articles in three U.S. newspapers (July 1992–January 2004)

		New York Times	Washington Post	Wall Street Journal	Average
ROK	Descriptive	-0.48	-0.50	-0.10	-0.36
	Evaluative	-0.21	-0.24	-0.19	-0.21
U.S.-ROK	Descriptive	-0.12	-0.12	0.05	-0.06
	Evaluative	-0.17	-0.13	-0.24	-0.18
DPRK	Descriptive	-0.72	-0.95	-0.57	-0.75
	Evaluative	-0.52	-0.91	-0.67	-0.70
U.S.-DPRK	Descriptive	-0.54	-0.74	-0.50	-0.59
	Evaluative	-0.72	-0.91	-0.89	-0.84
ROK-DPRK relations	Descriptive	-0.18	-0.28	-0.13	-0.20
	Evaluative	-0.14	-0.36	-0.31	-0.27
Average tone	Descriptive	-0.41	-0.52	-0.25	-0.39
	Evaluative	-0.35	-0.51	-0.46	-0.44

It is clear that the ROK was described and evaluated quite favorably during the study period, especially relative to the DPRK, which registered very negative tone scores (–0.75 for descriptive articles and –0.70 for evaluative articles, versus –0.36 and –0.21 for the ROK).[10] Likewise, U.S.-ROK relations fared much better than U.S.-DPRK relations in the eyes of the U.S. media. The average descriptive tone for the U.S.-ROK alliance was –0.06—an effectively neutral score—while the average descriptive tone for U.S.-DPRK relations was –0.59. The evaluative tones exhibit similar tendencies, at –0.18 for the U.S.-ROK bond—again, close to neutral—versus a very negative –0.84 for the U.S.-DPRK relationship. Indeed, in terms of both descriptive and evaluative articles, *the U.S.-ROK relationship received the most favorable coverage* of any focus category during the study period.

The manner in which the U.S. media evaluate each country—as opposed to America's *relationship* with that country—presents additional perspective on the U.S. media portrayal of events and their implications. While the average descriptive tone for ROK news (–0.36) was more negative than that for U.S.-ROK news (–0.06), the tone of evaluative paragraphs on these topics was very close: –0.21 and –0.18, respectively. The descriptive results suggest that for the most part, from the U.S. perspective, negative events in South Korea do not necessarily impact reportage on alliance-related matters. The preponderance of economic news during the study period, including news about the late-1990s financial crisis (see table 1.2), explains why this is likely the case. The very close evaluative scores for ROK and U.S.-ROK news demonstrate that the U.S.

media judge these topics similarly, although newspapers *evaluate* the U.S.-ROK relationship in slightly more negative terms than they *describe* events related to the relationship. Still, the fact that the U.S.-ROK relationship is the least negative focus category according to both measures of tone seems to suggest that the alliance has been in good shape for most of the study period.

In terms of descriptive articles, coverage of the DPRK was more negative than that of U.S.-DPRK relations (–0.75 versus –0.59). For evaluative articles, the opposite was true (–0.70 for DPRK news versus –0.84 for U.S.-DPRK news). In other words, the DPRK is *described* more negatively than U.S.-DPRK relations, illustrating Americans' deep-rooted negative view of the DPRK. Yet in evaluative terms, leading U.S. newspapers are much more critical of the U.S.-DPRK relationship than of the country itself. In addition, while the *Post*'s tone toward the DPRK is much more negative than that of the *Times* and the *Journal*, the evaluative tone toward U.S.-DPRK relations is quite similar across all three. These findings demonstrate that U.S. media not only view U.S.-DPRK relations very critically, but that they also exhibit significant agreement in their assessment of the relationship, including judgments on U.S. policy toward the DPRK and its nuclear programs, the principal topics covered within articles on the DPRK.

Evaluating article tone by issue type

Table 1.5 examines descriptive and evaluative articles about the Korean Peninsula, divided by issue category. Among descriptive articles, three very negative average ratings are readily apparent—those for domestic politics (–0.75), security (–0.71), and humanitarian/human rights issues (–0.71). While all three newspapers' descriptions of security and domestic politics vary little—they are all very negative—the variation on humanitarian/human rights issues is conspicuous, with the *Washington Post* being most negative at –0.97. Even though the other two newspapers do not replicate this very negative descriptive tone score, it remains noteworthy that a prominent U.S. newspaper (in this case, the *Post*) has portrayed the human rights issue even more negatively (in both descriptive and evaluative terms) than the security issue. When we averaged the descriptive tone scores for the three newspapers, humanitarian/human rights issues rated just as negatively as security issues (–0.71). These statistics provide some indication of the depth of American views about human rights in the DPRK.

The only issue that received neutral tone ratings—both descriptive and evaluative—was "general diplomacy," which we defined in our study as diplomacy other than that related to North Korea's WMD programs. With this important clarification established, it is understandable that articles about diplomacy on the Korean Peninsula would tend to be positive, since the period from 1992 to 2004 was characterized by ardent diplomatic activity, resulting in many agreements, including the North-South Basic Agreement, the inter-Korean summit, and high-level U.S.-DPRK exchanges toward the end of the Clinton administration.

Table 1.5 Across the Korean Peninsula: Average tone of descriptive and evaluative news articles in three U.S. newspapers, divided by issue category (July 1992–January 2004)

All Korean Peninsula		New York Times	Washington Post	Wall Street Journal	Average
Security	Descriptive	-0.68	-0.79	-0.66	-0.71
	Evaluative	-0.69	-0.89	-0.89	-0.82
Domestic politics	Descriptive	-0.79	-0.68	-0.77	-0.75
	Evaluative	-0.28	-0.47	-0.53	-0.43
Economy and trade	Descriptive	-0.15	-0.56	0.06	-0.22
	Evaluative	-0.15	-0.47	-0.13	-0.25
General diplomacy	Descriptive	0.18	0.24	-0.18	0.08
	Evaluative	0.03	0.04	-0.22	-0.05
Human rights issues	Descriptive	-0.58	-0.97	-0.59	-0.71
	Evaluative	-0.47	-1.00	-0.75	-0.74
Other	Descriptive	-0.48	-0.02	-0.05	-0.18
	Evaluative	-0.11	-0.02	-0.30	-0.14
Average tone	Descriptive	-0.42	-0.46	-0.37	-0.42
	Evaluative	-0.28	-0.47	-0.47	-0.41

On the majority of issues, the *Washington Post* was the most negative of the three newspapers. In particular, the *Post*'s descriptive and evaluative articles on economic and trade issues were far more negative than those of the other two newspapers. Yet the *Post* also published dramatically fewer articles on economic topics than did its counterparts; in the course of this study, the *Post* carried only 98 articles on such topics, while the *Times* and the *Journal* published 582 and 1,067 articles, respectively. Thus, it appears that the *Washington Post* will not cover an economic story related to the Korean Peninsula unless the story is a very negative, significant event—perhaps one so significant that it spills over into other issue areas. This is somewhat understandable given the *Post*'s politically focused audience in Washington and its preference for security, political, and diplomatic coverage (over the study period, the *Post* published 734 articles on security).

For news on the ROK and U.S.-ROK relations, as table 1.6 shows, general diplomacy was once again the most positive issue category, with an average evaluative tone of –0.15 and an average descriptive tone of 0.20, the most positive tone score for any issue in this survey. Human rights issues were rated the most negative among descriptive articles, but there were very few ROK-related articles on this issue—providing insufficient data points to draw any conclusions.

Table 1.6 South Korea: Average tone of descriptive and evaluative articles in three U.S. newspapers, divided by issue category (July 1992–January 2004)

ROK		New York Times	Washington Post	Wall Street Journal	Average
Security	Descriptive	-0.69	-0.32	-0.64	-0.55
	Evaluative	-0.67	-0.33	-0.79	-0.59
Domestic politics	Descriptive	-0.92	-0.57	-0.94	-0.81
	Evaluative	-0.34	-0.26	-0.59	-0.39
Economy and trade	Descriptive	-0.28	-0.71	0.02	-0.32
	Evaluative	-0.43	-0.50	-0.21	-0.38
General diplomacy	Descriptive	-0.04	0.64	0.00	0.20
	Evaluative	-0.47	0.53	-0.50	-0.15
Human rights issues	Descriptive	0.00	-1.00	-2.00	-1.00
	Evaluative	0.30	-0.83	-1.50	-0.68
Other	Descriptive	-0.75	-0.04	-0.10	-0.30
	Evaluative	-0.23	0.07	-0.15	-0.10
Average tone	Descriptive	-0.45	-0.33	-0.61	-0.46
	Evaluative	-0.31	-0.22	-0.62	-0.38

The tone on the issue of domestic politics varied greatly among newspapers, with the *Washington Post* registering the least negative coverage of ROK domestic politics. On average, each newspaper also exhibited a greater disparity (than for other issues) between descriptive and evaluative tone scores on the issue of domestic politics, with descriptive scores being more negative. The average descriptive tone for domestic politics was –0.81, whereas the average evaluative tone was –0.39. These figures suggest that the U.S. media assess ROK domestic politics in less negative terms than events might otherwise indicate. In other words, despite negative events in South Korean politics—including corruption and other political scandals—the U.S. media appear to have confidence in the durability of South Korean political institutions and democracy, as well as in the direction of domestic politics for most of the study years. In fact, during the study period,

South Korea not only saw the peaceful transfer of power to a civilian government but also witnessed shifts from the ruling party to the opposition party, all without any constitutional crisis.

The *Washington Post*'s coverage of economic and trade issues (–0.71 descriptive, –0.50 evaluative) was much more negative than that of either the *New York Times* (–0.28 descriptive, –0.43 evaluative) or the *Wall Street Journal* (0.02 descriptive, –0.21 evaluative). Once again, such a disparity may reflect the *Post*'s tendency to skip an economic story related to the Korean Peninsula unless it centers on a very negative, significant event. In addition, the newspapers showed an even greater degree of variation in tone—both descriptive and evaluative—in their economic and trade coverage than they did in their coverage of domestic politics. The significant variations in reportage and opinion among U.S. newspapers on economic and trade matters demonstrate the diverse portrayals of the ROK in American media.

As table 1.7 shows, human rights stories were the most negative of all DPRK-related stories, both in terms of descriptive tone (–0.96) and evaluative tone (–1.12). Given the fairly sizable number of articles that each newspaper published on this topic (52 on average), it seems clear that human rights is a significant component of U.S. media interest in North Korea. There is interesting variation among descriptive articles on this issue: the *Washington Post* was the most negative (–1.33), followed by the *New York Times* (–0.89) and the *Wall Street Journal* (–0.67). The *Post* also carried significantly fewer articles on human rights, and on DPRK news in general (402 DPRK-related articles in total, compared with 801 from the *Times* and 752 from the *Journal*). The newspapers' evaluative articles on human rights showed less variation, though on average they were more negative than their descriptive counterparts. That is, U.S. newspapers *evaluated* the issue of human rights in even more negative terms than they used to *describe* events. Once again, this finding seems to reflect how American people and policymakers view human rights in North Korea, an issue that energizes both internationalists on the left and religious conservatives on the right of the American political spectrum.

Security and domestic politics also received very negative descriptive and evaluative scores. Security is by far the most covered issue in DPRK news—the *Post* published 509 articles, the *Times* 491, and the *Journal* 199—while the domestic politics of North Korea was covered at a comparatively lower rate: about 23 articles per newspaper, on average, over the study period. On security, the *Times*' descriptive tone (–0.77) was less negative than that of the other two newspapers (–0.92 for the *Post* and –1.00 for the *Journal*). Evaluative tone scores on security were less varied and just slightly more negative than the scores of descriptive articles on the issue. This lack of significant difference, both among newspapers and between evaluative and descriptive tones, demonstrates that the U.S. press sees actual events and U.S. reaction to them as fairly congruous or appropriate, and again emphasizes the relative invariability of American opinion on this issue.

Table 1.7 North Korea: Average tone of descriptive and evaluative articles in three U.S. newspapers, divided by issue category (July 1992–January 2004)

DPRK		New York Times	Washington Post	Wall Street Journal	Average
Security	Descriptive	-0.77	-0.92	-1.00	-0.90
	Evaluative	-0.95	-1.06	-1.12	-1.04
Domestic politics	Descriptive	-0.92	-0.88	-0.89	-0.90
	Evaluative	-1.05	-0.96	-0.89	-0.97
Economy and trade	Descriptive	0.20	-0.44	0.35	0.04
	Evaluative	-0.14	-0.67	0.05	-0.25
General diplomacy	Descriptive	0.04	-0.19	-0.60	-0.25
	Evaluative	0.05	-0.48	-0.22	-0.22
Human rights issues	Descriptive	-0.89	-1.33	-0.67	-0.96
	Evaluative	-1.15	-1.29	-0.94	-1.12
Other	Descriptive	-0.53	0.33	1.25	0.35
	Evaluative	-0.73	0.11	-1.17	-0.59
Average tone	Descriptive	-0.48	-0.57	-0.26	-0.44
	Evaluative	-0.66	-0.72	-0.71	-0.70

Economy and trade issues were viewed most positively; average tone scores for the *Times* and the *Journal* are 0.20 and 0.35, respectively. The average tone of descriptive articles on this issue was 0.04, and the average evaluative tone was –0.25. While the positive descriptive tone may be linked to reports of economic progress in the DPRK, where events that provide glimmers of hope are newsworthy against the backdrop of a depressed economy, the more negative evaluative tone may reflect U.S. skepticism toward the efficacy of the DPRK's reforms and its economic relations with neighboring countries.

Interestingly, though, thus far we have observed significant agreement across the three newspapers' evaluations of DPRK security and human rights issues, they varied considerably on the issue of diplomacy, suggesting disagreement over the efficacy of American diplomatic approaches. With respect to diplomacy, the *Times* took a neutral descriptive tone (0.04), the *Post* was slightly negative (–0.19), and the *Journal* was decidedly negative (–0.60). It is noteworthy that the *Journal*—the newspaper with the fewest articles on this issue (only ten articles over more than ten years)—was the most negative. This may imply that its coverage of diplomacy functions in much the same way that the *Washington Post's* coverage of economic issues does—that is, for topics outside the newspaper's expertise or typical areas of focus, there is little coverage, triggered by only the most negative developments.

Analyzing U.S. coverage of the Korean Peninsula as a whole, we see that security persists as one of the most problematic issues for the U.S. media, ostensibly because of the DPRK's pursuit of nuclear weapons. More positive (and less negative) tones on other issues, such as economics, may imply that the United States and the ROK have foundations upon which to build a more robust relationship, quite apart from their partnership in countering the threat posed by the DPRK. In light of this, it may be constructive for Washington and Seoul to channel attention toward these other issues even as they formulate a cooperative response to the DPRK's provocations. In particular, the successful negotiation of the KORUS FTA (which, at the time of this writing, is pending legislative approval) could potentially strengthen the thus far security-based bilateral relationship.

In table 1.8, we examine whether there is any meaningful relationship between news attention and news sentiment. Our data suggest that for some subjects there does seem to be a relationship between the volume of coverage (number of articles) and its tone. North Korea's pursuit of WMD, human rights in the DPRK, and the Korean economic crisis all exhibit high negative correlations between news volume and tone ($P \leq .001$). That is, during the study period, a more negative tone is used to describe these particular subjects. This is not surprising given the media's negative bias and the nature of some of these subjects; it makes sense that news about the economic crisis would be negative and that a heightened sense of crisis would precipitate more reporting. Similarly, the subject of human rights is not usually newsworthy unless rights are violated. Other categories, however, such as general diplomacy, ROK-DPRK economic relations, and U.S.-ROK trade, showed a high positive correlation between news volume and tone.

Negative and positive correlations between media attention and sentiment (or tone) have important implications for public diplomacy, and perhaps even policy. In particular, categories that receive the most attention and are rated most negatively are the most problematic. As demonstrated in table 1.8, shifting attention and emphasis away from frequently covered negative issues (such as security) toward lesser-known positive ones (such as economic and cultural affairs) could be an effective public diplomacy strategy for South Korea, and could improve American perceptions of the nation. Although this would be a complex exercise,[11] as public diplomacy cannot be wholly divorced from newsworthy events or sound policy, these findings should be taken into account as Seoul seeks to improve its image in the United States. Pyongyang faces a much more difficult challenge, as the U.S. media tend to view North Korea in consistently negative terms, producing a fixed, unfavorable image of the nation. To change such monolithic coverage of the country, the DPRK should grant better access to the foreign correspondents who visit the country. As Caroline Gluck (a former BBC correspondent based in Seoul who has traveled repeatedly to the DPRK) points out in chapter 9 of this volume, North Korean officials "should use the opportunity of foreign media visits to tell the world their viewpoint, to show us a side of the country that rarely gets told, as they often complained about negative foreign reporting."

Table 1.8 Correlation between news volume and tone in three U.S. newspapers (July 1992–January 2004)

	Negative correlation	Positive correlation
Issue	Security and military (-.94***)	General diplomacy (.47***)
	Domestic politics (-.90***)	Arts/culture/religion (.52***)
	Economy and trade (-.81***)	
	Humanitarian/human rights issues (-.67***)	
	Social issues (-.34***)	
Subject	North Korea's WMD (including nuclear weapons and missiles) (-.92***)	ROK-DPRK economic relations (.66***)
	U.S. troops in South Korea (with protests not the focus) (-.83***)	ROK-U.S. trade (.15*)
	North Korea's arms trafficking/drug sales/smuggling (-.86***)	South Korean economy/industry (general) (.07*)
	South Korea's civic movement (-.96***)	
	Korean economic (financial) crisis (-.96***)	
	Human rights issues in North Korea (-.70***)	

Note: * $P \leq .05$
** $P \leq .01$
*** $P \leq .001$

Temporal Fluctuations

News attention over time, July 1992–January 2004

Having analyzed how the U.S. media cover the Korean Peninsula, both in terms of focus and tone, it is worth examining coverage trends over time. Figure 1.1 charts the number of articles that the three designated newspapers devoted to coverage of the Korean Peninsula over the period July 1992–January 2004. As expected, all three newspapers exhibit significant "spikes" in coverage around 1994, 1997, and 2002–2003. These periods of relatively high coverage correspond to major crises and their fallout—the first North Korean nuclear crisis, the Asian financial crisis, and the second North Korean nuclear crisis, respectively—lending credence to the notion of hot-spot journalism, which Karl Schoenberger discusses in chapter 2.

Figure 1.1 Coverage (number of articles) of South Korea in three U.S. newspapers (June 1992–January 2004)

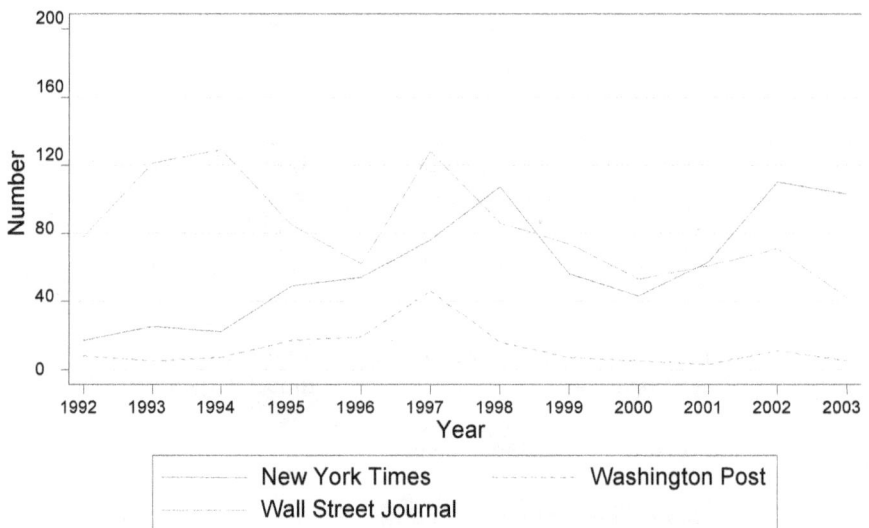

Note: y-axis scale is unified.

In relative terms, before 1997 the *Wall Street Journal* generated the most articles on the Korean Peninsula, followed by the *New York Times* and the *Washington Post*.[12] But after 1997 the *New York Times*' volume of articles on Korea-related issues rose to exceed that of the other two newspapers. For most of this time, the *Wall Street Journal* published the second highest number of articles, while the *Washington Post* retained its third-place ranking. An exception to this rank order occurred in 2002 and 2003, when the *Post* published a few more articles on Korea than the *Journal*. Given the *Post*'s relatively higher coverage of security and diplomatic issues, as well as U.S.-DPRK news, the increase during these years is not surprising. Figure 1.1 illustrates the extent to which the *New York Times* has outpaced the other two papers in its coverage of the Korean Peninsula in recent years.

Now we turn to examining changes in news attention and tone by focus and issue.

Changes in focus

Figure 1.2 shows changes over time in coverage of the ROK and U.S.-ROK relations. The graph enables us to make a number of compelling observations. First, the ROK has consistently received more coverage in the U.S. media than U.S.-ROK relations. During the study period, there is no single year when the relationship received more coverage than the country. Second, a major peak in ROK news occurred in 1997, reflecting the financial crisis. However, the sharp increase in coverage of ROK news during the financial crisis was not mirrored by a rise in coverage of the U.S.-ROK relationship. This suggests that the *New York Times*, the *Washington Post*, and the *Wall Street Journal* did not see the financial crisis in the context of the bilateral relationship—in contrast to some observers in South Korea. Third, we find a small peak in ROK-related news coverage in 2002, the inception of the peninsula's second nuclear crisis and the year of a South Korean presidential election that featured anti-American themes. In that election, South Korea chose a left-leaning, relatively unknown former human rights lawyer who, unlike his predecessors, did not have ties to the United States—a newsworthy fact in and of itself.

Turning to the two periods of nuclear crisis, we find that in 1994, contrary to expectations, the amount of U.S.-ROK coverage actually decreased from the previous year. In 2002, by contrast, there is a noticeable (though moderate) rise in the number of articles on U.S.-ROK relations. This increase suggests that the breaking nuclear crisis—perhaps in addition to the George W. Bush–Kim Dae-jung summit in 2001 and Bush's inclusion of the DPRK in the "axis of evil"—spurred greater scrutiny of the U.S.-ROK alliance and therefore more coverage. The increase in news attention might also be attributed to differences in how the crises affected the U.S.-ROK alliance: whereas the United States and the ROK were closely aligned on DPRK policy during the first nuclear crisis, they had disparate ideas about and policy approaches toward the second. The rise in coverage during the second standoff may speak to their involvement in seeking a resolution (through Six-Party Talks) while at the same time disagreeing on tactics. In sum, North Korea's nuclear ambitions have cast a spotlight on the diverging positions of Seoul and Washington and increased tensions in their alliance.

Figure 1.3 presents changes over time in U.S. news coverage of the DPRK and U.S.-DPRK relations. At times when the ROK received more news attention than U.S.-ROK relations, we observe that U.S.-DPRK relations received more news attention than the DPRK. Similarly, while coverage levels for the ROK fluctuated more than those for U.S.-ROK relations, figure 1.3 shows greater fluctuations in the coverage of U.S.-DPRK relations than of the nation itself.

23

Figure 1.2 Coverage (number of articles) of the ROK and U.S.-ROK relations in three U.S. newspapers (June 1992–January 2004)

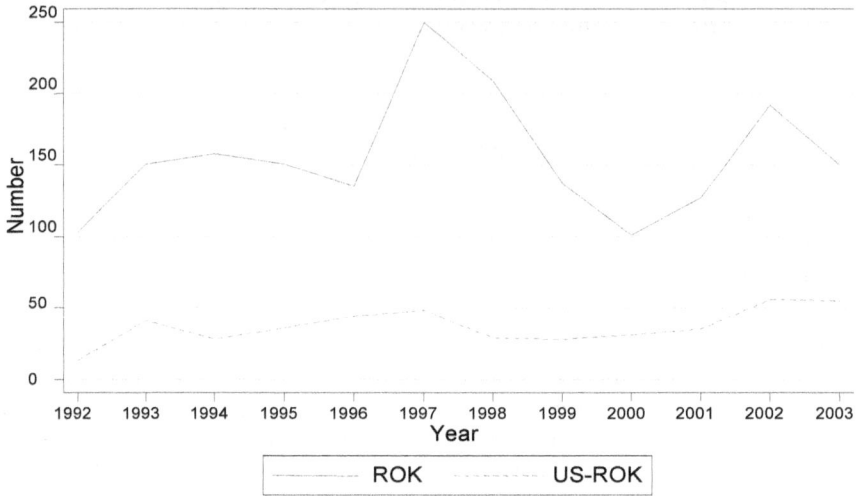

Figure 1.3 Coverage (number of articles) of the DPRK and U.S.-DPRK relations in three U.S. newspapers (June 1992–January 2003)

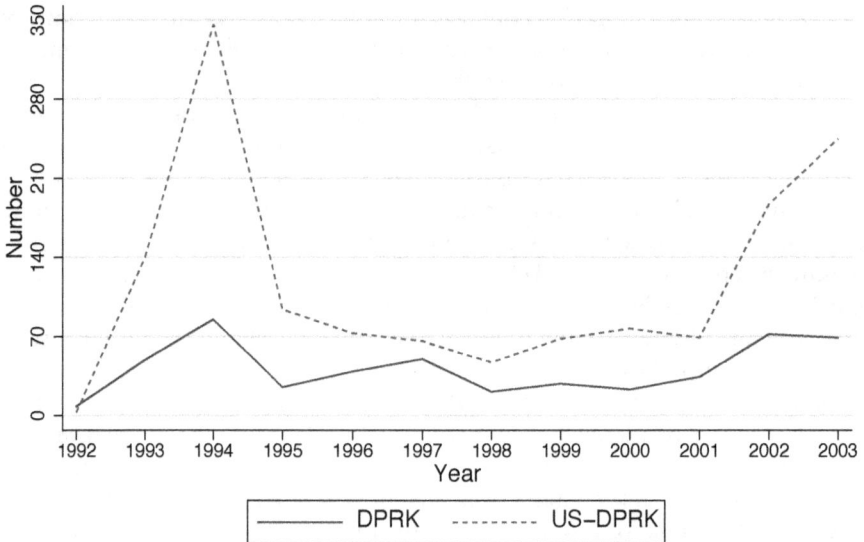

More distinctly than any other category, coverage of U.S.-DPRK relations exhibited two clear peaks, in 1994 and 2002–2003. These peaks indicate, once again, how much security-focused coverage dominates DPRK-related content and

Figure 1.4 Coverage (number of articles) of security-related issues on the Korean Peninsula in three U.S. newspapers (June 1992–January 2004)

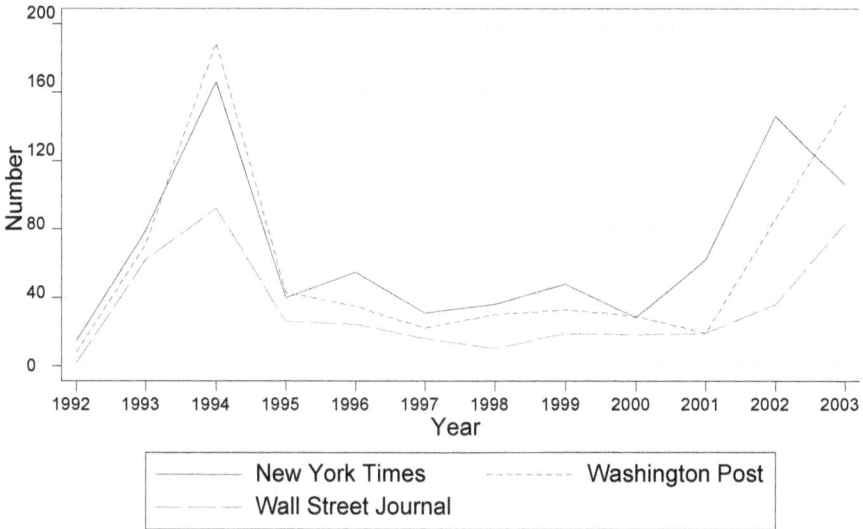

Note: y-axis scale is unified.

Figure 1.5 Coverage (number of articles) of economy- and trade-related issues on the Korean Peninsula in three U.S. newspapers (June 1992–January 2004)

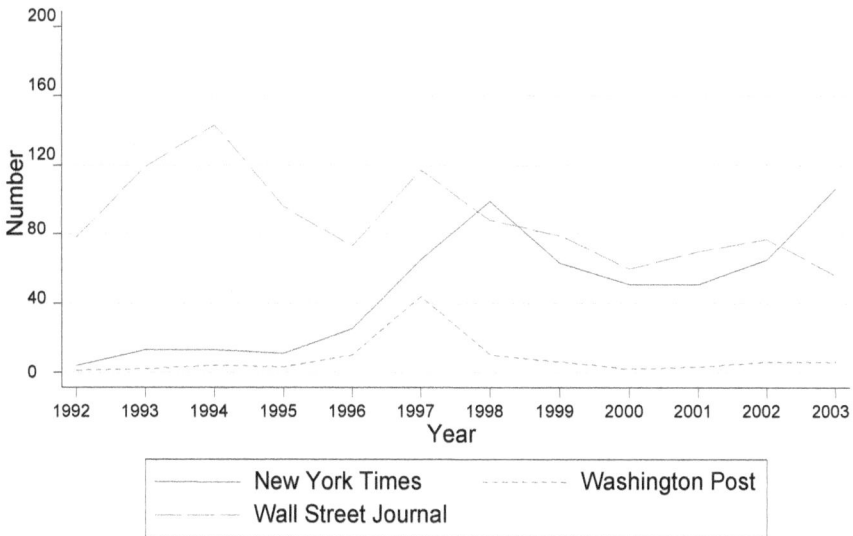

Note: y-axis scale is unified.

how widely the U.S. media perceive the nuclear crises as having a direct impact on the United States. Figure 1.3 shows that the highest peak in the coverage of U.S.-DPRK relations occurred in 1994, during the first nuclear crisis, although the monthly average is slightly greater during the second crisis. The second crisis may have received less coverage because the idea of a nuclear North Korea was not as new and therefore perhaps not as shocking (though just as dangerous) as it was during the first; these two qualities, novelty and surprise, tend to contribute to "newsworthiness." The relative size of coverage was also related to the environments in which the two crises occurred. In contrast to the first nuclear crisis, the second crisis had to compete with other compelling news, especially the wars in Iraq and Afghanistan. Also, according to *New York Times* journalist David E. Sanger, though the media reported on the events of the second crisis, President George W. Bush himself did not talk publicly about the steps North Korea was taking at the time. The White House's silence on North Korea—and contrasting volubility on Iraq—severely impeded the American media's ability to focus on North Korea and even gave rise to a journalistic conundrum on how to handle the story.[13]

The death of the North Korean leader Kim Il-sung in the summer of 1994 and concerns associated with it must have increased U.S. media coverage of the DPRK in that year. Apart from this extraordinary event and the two nuclear crises, however, DPRK-related issues have not received much attention in the U.S. media. Figure 1.3 clearly illustrates that in the time between nuclear crises, there was limited coverage of DPRK-related issues.

Changes in the issues addressed

Figures 1.4 and 1.5 depict fluctuations over time in coverage of the issues of security and economy/trade, respectively, which are two core news topics in the U.S. media. As expected, figure 1.4 shows two clear peaks during the nuclear crises. In general, though their individual coverage levels differed, the coverage of all three newspapers rose and fell in sync with events—with one exception. Although all three newspapers increased their coverage between 2001 and 2002—with the *Times* and the *Post* both recording dramatic increases—the *Times'* coverage dropped from 2002 to 2003 while that of the *Post* and the *Journal* continued to increase. The decrease at the *Times* may reflect competition for "column inches" as the second nuclear crisis fought for space with the U.S. war in Iraq and the new, broad, and consuming war on terror.

While the three newspapers' coverage of security issues is strikingly similar, there appears to be no trend for their coverage of economic and trade issues— except for a spike around the 1997 financial crisis. While the *Washington Post*'s interest in economic issues remained steadily low over the length of our study, the *New York Times'* interest has increased dramatically since 1996. Figure 1.5 illustrates these points and others; note that the *Post*'s only noticeable rise in economic coverage occurred during the 1997 financial crisis. This validates an earlier observation that, in large part, the *Post* only reports on economic issues in the case of dire events.

From figure 1.5 it is clear that the *Wall Street Journal* devotes the most coverage to economic and trade issues. The years in which it generated the greatest number of articles on the South Korean economy—1993–1994 and 1997—reflect the financial publication's natural interest in the ROK's high economic growth and its subsequent dramatic and sudden decline. Even though much of the *Journal's* coverage occurred during the first half of this study, there appears to be just as much coverage of the ROK economy during the second half, owing to the *New York Times'* significant increase in attention to this topic after 1998. Since that year, when the *Times'* economic coverage first overtook that of the *Journal*, the two newspapers have generally accorded comparable levels of coverage to economic and trade issues.

Changes in tone over time

We will now examine how the tone of U.S. media coverage has changed over time. We principally discuss evaluative articles, though we contrast these with descriptive articles when relevant. As previously discussed, the tone of evaluative and descriptive articles has a high rate of correlation (0.79). But points of divergence, where they do exist, may reveal important insights into U.S. coverage of the two Koreas.

Changes in tone across focus categories

Figure 1.6 depicts the tone of evaluative articles on ROK-related issues. While the tone of the *Wall Street Journal* and the *New York Times* is neutral for the first few years of the study, that of the *Washington Post* is positive, even above 1 in 1992. It is interesting to note that the *Post* exhibits conspicuously higher tone scores than the *Times* and the *Journal* over three periods: 1992–1993, 1998–1999, and 2001–2002. As we established in table 1.2, the *Post* devotes a higher percentage of its ROK-focused articles to domestic politics and diplomatic/security issues. The time periods cited are associated with South Korean election years (1992, 1997, and 2002) and positive diplomatic achievements on the Korean Peninsula. Over the course of these elections, South Korea witnessed the establishment of the first civilian government in thirty years and the first peaceful transfer of power from the ruling to the opposition party, indicative of a maturing democracy. On the diplomatic/security front, 1992 saw the normalization of relations between the ROK and China as well as the ROK-DPRK Joint Declaration of Denuclearization, and 1999 featured the Perry process, a high-profile, comprehensive review of U.S. policy toward North Korea, led by former secretary of defense William Perry. The improved tone of the *Times* and the *Journal* in 1998 and 1999 likely reflects a recuperating South Korea, the Asian economy that weathered the financial crisis most successfully.

Figure 1.6 Average evaluative tone of three U.S. newspapers' coverage of South Korea (June 1992–January 2004)

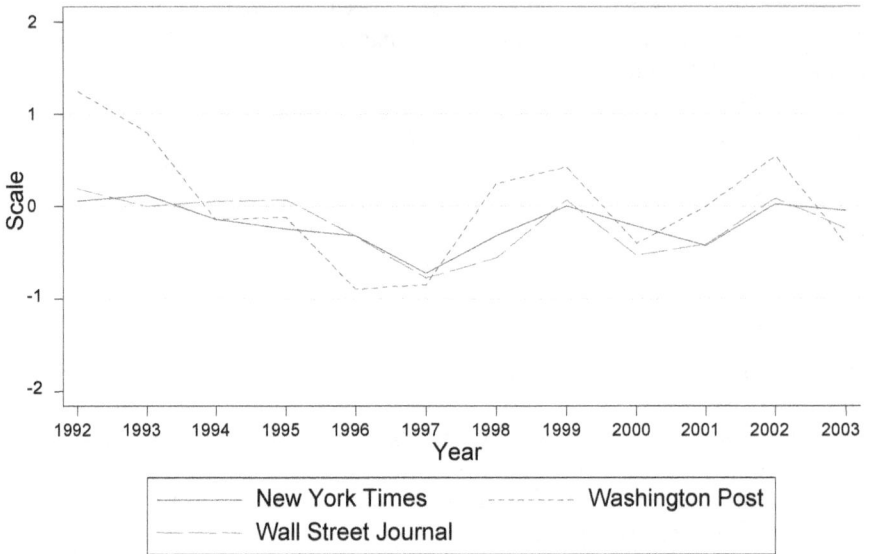

For articles on the ROK, the relatively negative tone scores of 2000 and improvements in 2001 and 2002 are more difficult to explain. Comparing the tone of descriptive and evaluative ROK-focused articles in 2000, it seems that the fairly positive descriptions of events related to the South's new approach toward the North were not matched by evaluative news content. This may reflect the American media's skepticism of the new ROK-DPRK relations. Improvements in the tone of both article types in 2002 were likely related to the presidential campaign and election of Roh Moo-hyun. While some in the United States worried how his election might affect the U.S.-ROK alliance, it appears that the U.S. media saw the election of a little-known politician as evidence of South Korea's maturing democracy.

In figure 1.6, it is interesting to note that while coverage of the ROK was aligned across the three newspapers, that of U.S.-ROK relations was not. That is, when one newspaper improves its tone, a second paper might do the opposite, as between 1996 and 1998. This divergence indicates that opinion on the U.S.-ROK relationship is more complex and varied than that on South Korea itself.

Figure 1.7 reveals a dynamic picture of the changing tone toward U.S.-ROK relations, which is generally more positive than that toward the ROK. It appears that 2001 was a critical year for U.S. media evaluation of the U.S.-ROK alliance. From 2000 to 2001, all three newspapers showed a decline in tone, though to starkly different degrees. The *Wall Street Journal*'s tone fell slightly, becoming neutral; the *New York Times'* tone turned moderately negative; and the *Washington Post's* tone dropped significantly, becoming highly negative (approximately −2, the most negative rating on this scale). This drop occurred despite the improved tone of *Journal* and *Post* articles on the ROK between 2000 and 2001. It is likely that friction caused by differing policy views on North Korea between the administrations of Kim Dae-jung and the newly elected George W. Bush informed this downward turn. The fact that the *Washington Post's* score is the most negative supports this view, because the two allies disagreed over security and political issues, both major news items for the *Post*. That there were no significant economic or trade-related disputes between presidents Bush and Kim similarly explains the smaller change in tone of the financial-focused *Journal*.

Figure 1.7 Average evaluative tone of three U.S. newspapers' coverage of U.S.-ROK relations (June 1992–January 2004)

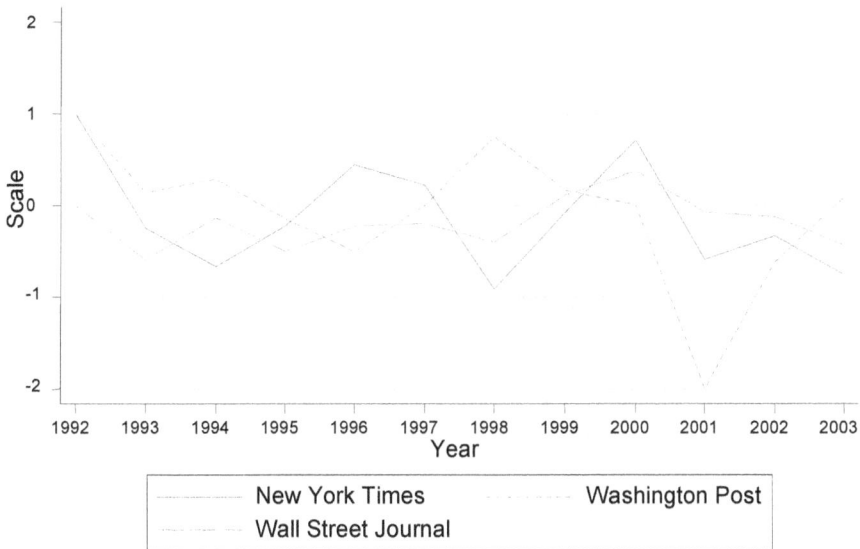

Figure 1.8 illustrates changes in U.S. media tone toward the DPRK, and figure 1.9 does the same for U.S.-DPRK relations. The most glaring contrast with the corresponding figures for the ROK is that the tone is never positive in the case of the DRPK—with one noteworthy exception, in 2000, that we will discuss. It is also interesting to note that overall newspaper evaluations of U.S.-DPRK relations are similar, while those of the DPRK diverge. Recall that for South Korea, the opposite was true—the tone of U.S. coverage of the country was similar across the three newspapers, while that of U.S.-ROK relations diverged. If we also remember that, in terms of news attention, the ROK received much more

than did U.S.-ROK relations—while the opposite was true for the DPRK—it becomes apparent that tone trends align across newspapers for focus categories that receive more coverage. Less covered categories—for example, those not driven by clear, easily interpreted events—tend to generate a greater variance in tone across newspapers.

Figure 1.8 Average evaluative tone of three U.S. newspapers' coverage of North Korea (June 1992–January 2004)

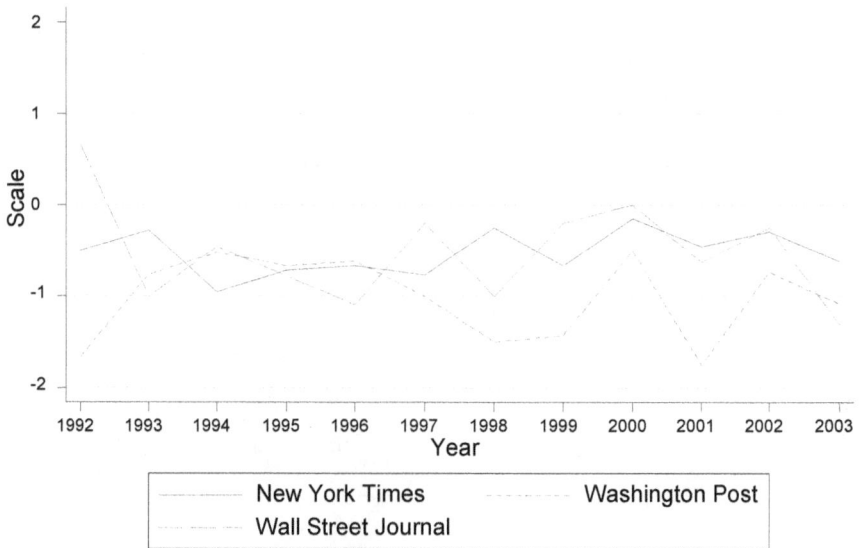

As noted earlier, the single year in which DPRK-related coverage registered a positive tone was 2000 (see figure 1.9). This year—when evaluative articles in the *Journal* and *Post* were positive and those in the *Times* were neutral—marks one of the most dramatic changes in tone on DPRK-related news. It likely reflects developing views—spurred by high-level U.S.-DPRK meetings (particularly Marshall Cho's visit to Washington and then–secretary of state Madeleine Albright's return visit to Pyongyang) and the historic inter-Korean summit—that North Korea might graduate from being a "rogue regime" to becoming a functioning member of the international community, with a normalized relationship to the United States. Interestingly enough, the events of 2000 produced a much greater spike in tone for U.S.-DPRK relations than for ROK-DPRK relations. This suggests that, from the perspective of the American media, the events of 2000 had a more dramatic impact on U.S.-DPRK relations or—at the very least—that these were more relevant to an American audience than inter-Korean relations. The precipitous decline in tone from 2000 to 2001 suggests the quelling of this optimism, as the recently inaugurated Bush administration markedly departed from the Clinton administration's policy approach, expressing strong skepticism that inter-Korean engagement would yield any real change or positive result while refusing to engage North Korea. These actions effectively nullified the two U.S.-DPRK communiqués signed in Washington in 2000.

Figure 1.9 Average evaluative tone of three U.S. newspapers' coverage of U.S.-DPRK relations (June 1992–January 2004)

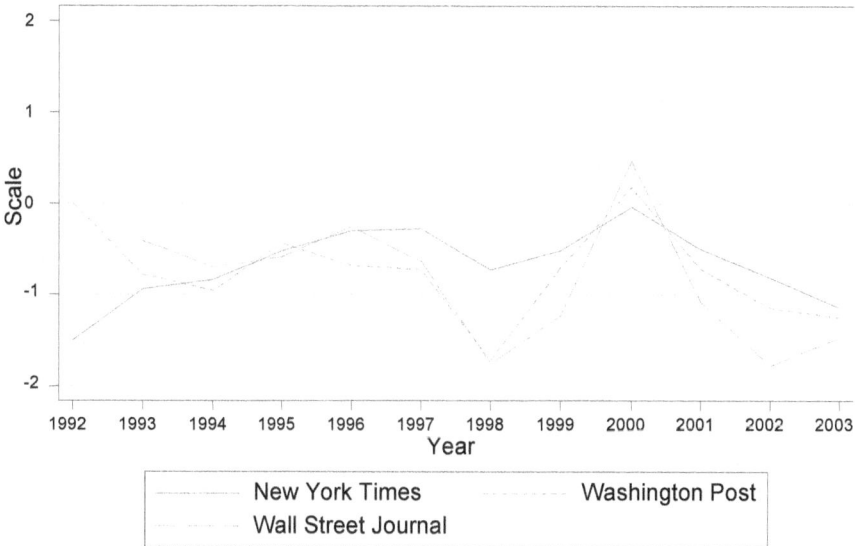

In contrast, the tone of DPRK-related articles more or less converged in the years 1994–1996. The tone of articles focused on the DPRK stayed relatively flat while those on U.S.-DPRK relations steadily improved. Events of 1998, most notably the growing recognition of famine in North Korea and the North's provocative missile launch over Japanese territory, seem to have stratified the newspapers' tones toward the DPRK and U.S.-DPRK relations. Figure 1.8 depicts the very different evaluative responses to the DPRK in this year; figure 1.9 illustrates the same for U.S.-DPRK relations, while showing that the drop in tone was more gradual for the *Times* than for the *Post* and the *Journal*. Perhaps the *New York Times* viewed the United States' and international aid response to North Korea's famine as a positive development that might produce goodwill and lead to future opening, while the *Post* and *Journal* may have focused on security issues, such as the DPRK's missile test. It is also interesting to note that the negative tone toward the U.S.-DPRK relationship in 1998 was nearly matched in the last few years of the study (from 2000 to 2003, including the first years of the present nuclear crisis). While the *Wall Street Journal* has tended to be the most negative news source, the last year of data, 2003, includes very negative assessments of the U.S.-DPRK relationship across all newspapers. The second nuclear crisis broke in October 2002, but significant events that deepened the crisis—including North Korea's withdrawal from the Nuclear Non-Proliferation Treaty and the removal of International Atomic Energy Agency inspectors from the Yongbyon nuclear facility, as well as intense debate on how to resolve the nuclear crisis—all occurred in 2003. It seems that the American media came to share a pessimistic view of the North Korean nuclear crisis unfolding as the United States was engaged in the war on terror.

Meanwhile, descriptive articles on U.S.-DPRK relations correlate much more closely than for any other focus category. This reveals that while there may be more U.S. coverage devoted to the ROK, there is greater consensus on the U.S.-DPRK relationship than on any other topic. Earlier, we established that U.S.-DPRK coverage appears more event-driven than that of other focus categories, most notably during the time of the two nuclear crises. It makes sense that events surrounding the threat of nuclear weapons—certainly an extreme threat—would elicit similar descriptive coverage across U.S. newspapers, even among newspapers of varying ideological stripes. In terms of variance among evaluative articles over time, the ROK and U.S.-DPRK relations are both noteworthy for the relatively uniform trends in opinion exhibited for each focus category.

Changes in tone across issues

Figure 1.10 illustrates that over the course of this study, evaluative articles across the three U.S. newspapers agree that security on the Korean Peninsula is not ideal, remaining "somewhat negative" (–1 to 0) for the most part. But even during the first nuclear crisis in 1993 and 1994, none of the newspapers' evaluative tones fell below –1. That the U.S. media response to the first nuclear crisis was less negative than to the second can be attributed to a variety of factors, including general U.S.-ROK agreement on the appropriate diplomatic approach to the situation and the relative lack of concern over the North's potential connections to global terrorism in a post-9/11 world. In sharp contrast, the second crisis has been marked by policy differences between the United States and the ROK, heated debate on the issue within the United States, and concern over a possible transfer of nuclear materials or technology to terrorist groups. Our findings support the fractious U.S. opinion of the second crisis. As figure 1.10 illustrates, the articles on security-related matters are in close agreement during the first nuclear crisis; after, 2002 marks the greatest divergence, with the more conservative *Wall Street Journal* registering the most negative tone.

The divergence in tone among newspapers in 2000 indicates disagreement over the anticipated effects of nascent ROK-DPRK rapprochement on the security situation, as well as high-level U.S.-DPRK meetings. In figure 1.10, we see that during 2000, the *New York Times'* tone toward security remained relatively flat, whereas that of the *Wall Street Journal* and the *Washington Post* showed marked improvement. This is interesting given that, of the three major U.S. newspapers in this study, the *Times* devoted the most coverage to ROK-DPRK issues (10.8 percent, as shown in table 1.1). Figure 1.10 shows lack of agreement on the Korean summit and its impact on the security situation in the peninsula.

Figure 1.10 Average evaluative tone of three U.S. newspapers' coverage of security issues (June 1992–January 2004)

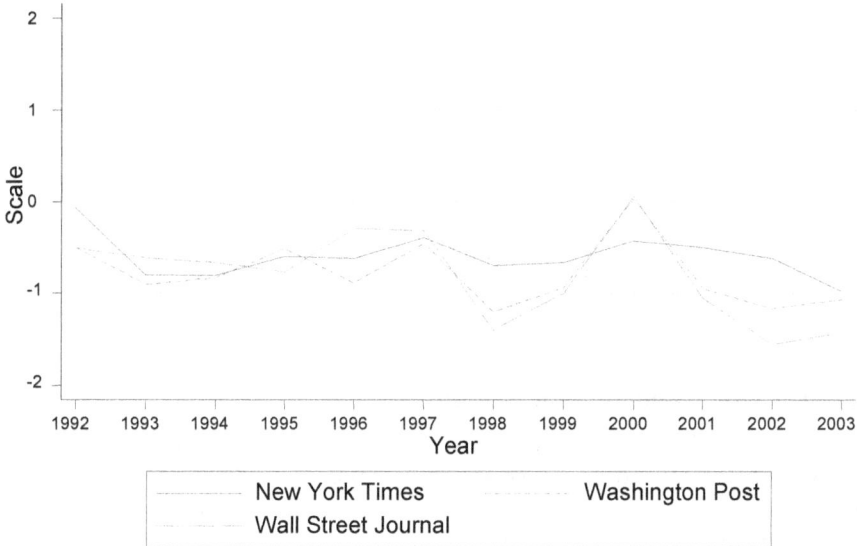

From 1992 through the eruption of the Asian financial crisis in 1997, the newspapers' evaluations of economic and trade issues varied little, as figure 1.11 shows. After that year, while the *Times* and the *Journal* continued to register similarly neutral tones, the *Post*'s tone took more exaggerated turns, rising into positive territory in 1998 and 2000, then dropping precipitously in 2001 to –2, the most negative tone rating on this scale. The *Post*'s evaluative tone exhibited similarly dramatic shifts in 2002 and 2003. All of these turns, except the one in 1998, were similarly reflected in the newspaper's descriptive articles. As discussed earlier, the *Post* tends to devote relatively little coverage to economic events on the Korean Peninsula, publishing articles only on those stories that are particularly timely or very negative. In 2001, a year in which South Korea reported slower than expected growth and experienced some relatively minor U.S.-ROK trade disputes, it remains uncertain exactly what event elicited such negative coverage from the *Post*, even as the *Journal* and *Times* coverage remained only slightly negative.

Figure 1.11 Average evaluative tone of three U.S. newspapers' coverage of economy and trade issues (June 1992–January 2004)

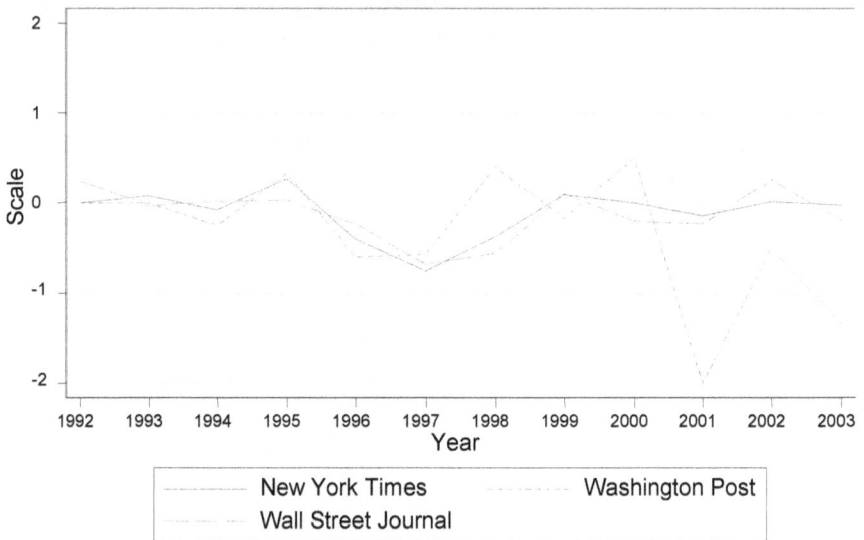

Further Discussion and Implications

This chapter details U.S. media attention and attitudes toward ROK- and DPRK-related news over eleven eventful years. As a whole, U.S. newspapers were fairly balanced in the amount of coverage they devoted to North versus South Korea. Security and economic issues in both took top priority. Yet we find crucial differences in the U.S. media coverage of ROK and DPRK news. South Korea itself received more news attention than did its relationship with the United States, with U.S. interest in economic and trade issues driving coverage. This finding suggests that the ROK, as a major trading partner, has importance to the United States beyond the security alliance; indeed, the alliance is not the primary basis for American interest in the country.

For DPRK-related news, by contrast, the U.S.-DPRK relationship featured far more frequently than did the DPRK itself (a finding partially due to information barriers, as the contributors to this book discuss in greater detail). Meanwhile, nearly three-fourths of this news related to security matters. American interest in North Korea is tethered to U.S. government responses, which are most often precipitated by security-related provocations. Across newspapers, similar percentages of DPRK-related content devoted to security issues further indicate that North Korea is primarily viewed as a security problem. It is thus apparent from our findings that the U.S. media—and by extension the U.S. public—see the ROK and the DPRK through very different lenses.

Differences across the three newspapers were revealing. Over the study period, the *Wall Street Journal* devoted more than two-thirds of its coverage to ROK-related issues, while the *Washington Post* devoted the majority of its coverage to DPRK-related issues. The *New York Times* showed more balance in its coverage of the Korean Peninsula. These differences may be explained by the newspapers' focuses. While the *Journal* is primarily concerned with economic and financial news, the *Post* concentrates on political events and security issues, providing scant coverage of economic issues. The *Times* attempts to cover both politics and economics in a thorough fashion. As a result, when we discover that the majority of U.S. coverage of the ROK is economic in nature, it makes sense that the *Journal* publishes more articles on the ROK than the *Post*. The *Times* occupies the middle ground, tending toward the *Journal*. Similarly, because an overwhelming majority of DPRK news covers security issues, it is predictable that the *Post* accords a higher percentage of its overall coverage to North Korea. Within types of coverage, the ROK and the U.S.-ROK relationship both yielded a relatively high number of special features (a descriptive article type), while the U.S.-DPRK relationship claimed the greatest amount of evaluative coverage (which is strongly associated with security/military issues), indicating a prolonged and heated policy debate over that relationship.

In light of tensions in the U.S.-ROK security alliance in the latter years of this study, it is important to note that this was the most positively portrayed focus category on average, indicating that the alliance was an important, favored aspect of U.S. interaction with the peninsula during much of the study period. In fact, news about the alliance registered a neutral descriptive tone, whereas news about the ROK carried a more negative descriptive tone.

In sharp contrast, U.S.-DPRK news recorded the most negative tone ratings of any focus category. The three newspapers' scores showed little variation, suggesting that the U.S. media were fairly unified in their portrayal of U.S.-DPRK relations. Across the newspapers' tone scores for DPRK issues, human rights was the most negative, even more negative than security and domestic politics. This is hardly surprising given that some humanitarian organizations have named North Korea as one of the world's foremost human rights offenders. While security may be the essential component of the North Korea problem from the U.S. perspective, it is the human rights issue that elicits exceptionally strong emotions. As a result, this issue rated more negatively in evaluative than descriptive articles.

Within DPRK news, security—which inspired far more coverage than human rights—was the second most negative issue. On the one hand, the lack of significant difference on security, both among newspapers and between evaluative and descriptive articles, demonstrates that the U.S. press sees actual events and U.S. reaction to them as fairly congruous or appropriate. On the other hand, more negative evaluative than descriptive articles on the DPRK economy may reflect U.S. skepticism of North Korea's economic relations with its neighbors (South Korea and China) and the efficacy of its reforms.

Taking into account U.S. newspaper coverage of the Korean Peninsula, we see that security is persistently one of the most troublesome areas from the perspective of the U.S. media, ostensibly owing to the DPRK's pursuit of nuclear weapons, its missile proliferation, and the impact of these threats on the U.S.-ROK alliance. More positive (and less negative) tones on other issues, such as economics, may imply that the United States and the ROK have foundations on which to build a more robust relationship, separate from their military partnership in countering the DPRK threat. The variation in news tone by issue allows us to discern the relative degree to which each issue area challenges the public image of both Koreas in the United States, thus providing what can be considered a clear, ordered list of public diplomacy priorities.

An analysis of the relationship between news attention and news sentiments across focus, issue, and subject category enables us to better understand which categories are most problematic. In other words, which categories receive high volumes of very negative coverage? These categories deserve the most attention from policymakers and practitioners of public diplomacy. On the other hand, those categories associated with high news volume and a positive tone may be viewed as starting points for additional cooperation. Data show that North Korean WMD, human rights in North Korea, and the Asian economic crisis all exhibit high negative correlations between news volume and descriptive tone. Subjects such as general diplomacy and the South Korean economy show a high positive correlation between news volume and tone. In essence, these findings suggest that public diplomacy efforts may attempt to channel U.S. media attention to subjects that foster more favorable images of South Korea. However, achieving such a positive perspective will be much more difficult for North Korea if it ever attempts to pursue such an end, given that the U.S. media view of the country as a whole is not only negative but also widely shared.

A temporal analysis of news attention and tone for the specified categories provides additional insights. All three newspapers exhibit significant spikes in coverage around 1994, 1997, and 2002–2003. These periods of relatively high coverage correspond to major crises and their fallout—namely, the first North Korean nuclear crisis, the Asian financial crisis, and the second North Korean nuclear crisis. The U.S. media's attention to these "bad news" stories confirms their negativity bias.

It is worth noting that the highest peak in coverage of U.S.-DPRK relations occurred in 1994, during the first crisis. Some might have expected the highest peak to occur during the second nuclear crisis, since it featured an additional element of complexity, unfolding as it did in the midst of the U.S. war on terror. During this period, there was paramount concern over the nexus between WMD-proliferating states and terrorists. Yet, a greater volume of coverage of U.S.-DPRK relations in 1994 may be associated with the "newsworthiness" of the first nuclear crisis; by the time of the second nuclear crisis, North Korea had gained the reputation of being an intractable problem. At the same time, as the chapters in this book clearly show, the extent of media attention must be weighed against competition from other stories at a given time. In this case, the North Korean story had to compete with other major events, especially the Iraq war. Simply put, in 1994 North Korea may have been a hot-spot story, but this had ceased to be the case by 2002 and 2003. During the second North Korean nuclear crisis, Iraq was the hot spot, which strongly influenced media coverage.

The second nuclear crisis prompted more variation in coverage among the three newspapers than the first. This is likely because the second crisis has been marked by significant policy differences between the United States and the ROK, as well as concern over the transfer of nuclear technology to terrorist groups. As a result, the second crisis produced more contending views and approaches toward the North, a divergence that is reflected in our findings.

With respect to the changed security environments, news about both U.S.-ROK and U.S.-DPRK relations became more negative during the second crisis. This finding indicates that the U.S. media viewed the second nuclear standoff more critically than the first because of concern over the possible linkages between the North's nuclear program and global terrorism, as well as policy discord between the United States and the ROK. Even so, the deterioration of the U.S.-DPRK relationship is not surprising—throughout the study period, it has been portrayed and assessed as highly conflict-ridden. More significant is the finding that news about U.S.-ROK relations became very negative during the second nuclear standoff. During the first crisis, the media did not consider the U.S.-ROK relationship to be especially unfavorable, but its news tone became highly negative during the second crisis, underscoring the two allies' policy rift over the North. This finding supports a prevailing argument that the divergent perception of and policy approach to North Korea have created a schism in the U.S.-ROK alliance.[14]

In terms of tone over time, it is worth revisiting the case of the ROK and the U.S.-ROK relationship. While the three newspapers' coverage generally followed the same tone trends for the ROK (a category shown to be highly responsive to events), U.S.-ROK coverage was marked by disparate trends. This divergence among newspapers indicates more complex views on the U.S.-ROK relationship than on South Korea itself. It is likewise notable that U.S.-ROK relations exhibited positive tone scores in nearly every year until 2001, after which scores were either negative or neutral. In this critical year, all three newspapers showed a decline in tone, though to starkly different degrees. Friction caused by differing policy views between the Kim Dae-jung and Bush administrations informed this downward turn.

New administrations have now taken office in Seoul and Washington, yet the North Korean nuclear crisis and domestic political constraints persist. It remains to be seen whether the U.S.-ROK alliance will become less conflict-ridden, as presidents Lee Myung-bak and Barack Obama have proclaimed.

Notes

[1] Other important data issues—such as sampling criteria, coding procedures, and validity and reliability—are not included here due to space limitations.

For more information on these issues, see chapter 2 in Gi-Wook Shin, *One Alliance, Two Lenses: U.S.-Korea Relations in a New Era* (Stanford, CA: Stanford University Press, 2009).

[2] The data we collected represent a total of 5,122 articles, but we excluded those not relevant to this chapter.

[3] Articles were divided into five "focus" categories: (1) ROK, (2) U.S. relations with the ROK, (3) DPRK, (4) U.S. relations with the DPRK, and (5) inter-Korean relations.

[4] It is not coincidental that two major financial papers, the *Wall Street Journal* and the *Financial Times*, have full bureaus in Seoul, while other papers are closing their offices there.

[5] We used the following categories to code the primary issue of each article or headline: (1) "security/military issues," (2) "domestic politics," (3) "economy/trade," (4) "general diplomacy," (5) "humanitarian/human rights issues," (6) "social issues," (7) "science and technology," (8) "arts/culture/religion," (9) "sports," and (10) "other."

[6] Note that domestic politics was a major issue in the U.S. press coverage of South Korea in the 1980s, when Koreans were fighting for democracy.

[7] For example, see the U.S.-ROK Strategic Forum "The Search for a Common Strategic Vision: Charting the Future of the US-ROK Security Partnership," codirected by G. John Ikenberry, Chung-in Moon, and Mitchell Reiss (Nautilus Institute Policy Forum Online, March 5, 2008), http://www.nautilus.org/fora/security/08018USROKForum.html.

[8] See Donald A. L. Macintyre, chapter 6 in this volume, for the problems of using defector testimony as a source of information on the DPRK.

[9] We determined article tone as mechanically as possible. First, we determined whether each paragraph in an article was either descriptive or evaluative. Subsequently, we coded each paragraph "positive," "negative," or "neutral" in accordance with the principles described earlier. In computing an article's descriptive news tone, we tallied the number of positive and negative descriptive paragraphs. If the proportion of positive (or negative) descriptive paragraphs exceeded 75 percent of all descriptive paragraphs, we determined the article's descriptive tone to be "primarily positive (or negative)," and we assigned a score of 2 (or –2). If the proportion of positive (or negative) paragraphs fell between 60 percent and 75 percent, we coded an article's descriptive tone as "somewhat positive (or negative)," and we assigned a score of 1 (or –1). We determined other articles to be "mixed/neutral," and we assigned them a score of 0. In order to avoid determining an article's tone based on inadequate information, we did not code an article's descriptive tone if fewer than three descriptive paragraphs were present. We assessed evaluative tone in the same fashion.

[10] It is worth recalling that these tone scores were derived from 630 articles about the ROK, in comparison to only 171 articles about the DPRK.

[11] See chapter 12, by David Straub, for a discussion of challenges in public diplomacy.

[12] Over the period of study, the three publications track remarkably closely on news attention in terms of the number of words devoted to the Koreas. The *Washington Post* published the fewest articles, meaning that it published the most words per article, on average.

[13] See David E. Sanger's remarks on this conundrum in chapter 11 of this volume. In fact, U.S. government officials were the primary source of the story for 40 percent of articles on U.S.-DPRK relations and 34 percent of articles on North Korea's WMD program.

[14] See Derek Mitchell, ed., *Strategy and Sentiment: South Korean Views of the United States and the U.S.-ROK Alliance* (Washington D.C.: Center for Strategic and International Studies, 2004), 107; "U.S.-Korea Relations: Opinion Leaders Seminar" (Korea Economic Institute, Washington D.C., July 2003).

Reporting on South Korea

A protester waves a U.S. flag at an anti-American demonstration in Seoul. *Credit:* Reuters/Lee Jae Won.

Hot-Spot Journalism:
The Problem with Sustainable Coverage
of the Korean Peninsula

Karl Schoenberger

When it comes to studying the behavior of the foreign press corps and their masters back home, I subscribe to the "hot-spot" theory. The hot spot to which I refer is the superintense focus that the U.S. and global news media train on a single international story, whether it be a war or a humanitarian crisis or a natural catastrophe in a distant land. Hot-spot journalism is transitory by nature; it can be compared, in the domestic arena, with the obsession over a titillating crime story or a celebrity scandal, but it takes place on a grander scale and involves stories of historic significance. The hot-spot foreign story tends to be covered almost to the exclusion of all other events of the day—particularly when little else of note is happening in the rest of the world that might compete for attention. Such a story is usually embraced with a vengeance and then dropped like a stone when a new hot spot arises elsewhere on the globe, trumping its predecessor's salacious appeal. Violence—or at least the impression of violence and a premonition of doom—tends to be the key ingredient. Regime change, as in the case of South Korea's transition from dictatorship to democracy, hits the jackpot.

The main drawback of this school of journalism is that its practitioners often fail to follow through on the aftershocks of the stories they cover. Further, they ignore significant new developments that take place after the hot spot has gone dark. Instead, hot-spot journalists prefer to revisit the scene at anniversary dates. The ten-year anniversary of Britain's handover of Hong Kong to the People's Republic of China provides a case in point. I attended that historically symbolic event in 1997 and can attest to the fact that it was a hot spot of British imperial proportions, distinguished by pomp and circumstance and a dearth of breaking news. The 2007 commemoration was an artificial occasion celebrating a nonevent. The real story of the Hong Kong handover, by contrast, took place behind the scenes as Beijing dashed hopes for promised autonomy and democratic reform in an insidious corruption of the Territory's Basic Law. With only desultory coverage, the story oozed out quietly over the past decade, overshadowed by business news about China's economic boom.

More than two decades ago, South Korea was changed forever by the fall of a military dictator and the eruption of energizing public rage. The pace of real-time news during that tumultuous period was blistering, and anniversary

43

commemorations of that turning point in history were far more relevant than the firework displays in Hong Kong. Nevertheless, I fear that the post-hot-spot syndrome in news coverage has shortchanged not only the people of Korea but also readers and audiences in the United States.

Coverage of the Korean Peninsula appears to align well with the international media's track record on covering—or not covering—important news. The pattern is one of excess and neglect. In the late 1980s, during its dramatic transition from despotism to fledgling democracy, South Korea was a pyrotechnic hot spot enjoying devoted scrutiny from a legion of foreign journalists. The daily print photos and television images fed back to the watching world showed student mobs hurling kerosene bottle-bombs that set riot police on fire, and volleys of pepper-gas spray fired in response. South Korea was a smoke-shrouded tableau—what we now call "eye candy"—and those dramatic images excited editors and enthralled media consumers.

I was one of many foreign journalists in South Korea at that time, covering the events from Tokyo, where I was a correspondent for the *Los Angeles Times*. We knew the procedure, having followed the steps many times before. When we reporters learned of a planned demonstration, we would rush to the battle scene, typically riding taxis to "Yonsei Beach," the grassy railroad embankment opposite the main gate of Yonsei University. Below this outdoor press gallery, we observed students engaging in the ritual confrontations with police that kept the story alive long after tyranny was on the run and the focus had shifted to political reform. The scene unfolding before international spectators had the air of a civil war battle reenactment. This diorama was staged with a phalanx of blue-clad riot police in Darth Vader helmets and gas masks facing off against a ragtag confederacy of student rebels charging and retreating, taunting the cops, many of whom were themselves former radical students serving out their mandatory military service. On cue, gangs of plainclothes goons—the so-called grabbers—would dance into the fray like Keystone Cops, chasing the protesters and nabbing the slower ones. They were conspicuous in their gray football helmets, which added a certain risibility to the drama.

My intent here is not to demean the crucial importance of antigovernment protests in toppling the Chun Doo-hwan regime and drawing the international pressure that helped to bring about historic change in South Korea. Though most of these demonstrations were peaceful, some did turn violent; in both cases, the presence and participation of ordinary citizens had a powerful influence on events. Rather, my point is that the hot-spot pattern of news coverage acted to skew perceptions about Korea and its people. It was at once a service and a disservice to Koreans. Most Americans would have been surprised to learn that such mayhem produced a remarkably low death toll. In a seemingly rough and pugnacious society, the sanctity of human life was a deeply rooted value. Nevertheless, the images of hotheaded, brawling Koreans increased the intensity of media coverage.

It could be argued that foreign reporters on the scene with their cameras and notebooks further elevated the intensity of the actors on the stage. This classic phenomenon in hot-spot journalism and many other fields is known as the Heisenberg effect, after the well-known phenomenon in physics. Heisenberg's uncertainty principle holds that the mere observation of a physical particle alters its position and makes its behavior unpredictable.[1] It is equally true that the human actors in these situations can intentionally manipulate the journalists to suit their own aims. The result is a distortion of reality, but an entertaining distortion that also can bring international attention—and sometimes influence a nation's destiny for the better. Hot spots are not all bad.

Most of the foreign journalists packed up and left for better hunting grounds not long after the closing ceremony of the Seoul Olympic Games, leaving audiences to guess what happened to the progress of a nascent democracy. Subsequent swarm coverage of the trouble in Beijing's Tiananmen Square in 1989 and of the breathtaking events in Moscow and Eastern Europe thereafter reduced the Korea story to a flickering memory. Koreans were left to sort out their future without the blinding camera lights of voyeuristic correspondents. As it happened, South Korea's road to democracy was successful, but the journey was essentially off the radar for the U.S. news media.

Nuclear Korea; or, How I Learned to Stop Worrying and Love the Bomb

In recent years, coverage of the North Korean nuclear weapons crisis has showcased the America media's limited capacity to focus on more than one thing at a time. This failing was largely a reflection of foreign policy dysfunction in the Bush administration, but that is not the only explanation.

The North Korean situation has received consistent and insightful coverage by a small cadre of journalists with expertise on nuclear proliferation, Northeast Asia, or both. But how are these stories presented when media attention is diverted, say, to the Middle East? In the inevitable ebb and flow of events, a story flares up and then goes dark, which means it does not always merit coverage. But sometimes, when critical events do occur, they are edged off the front page where they belong and are thereafter relegated to the back of the section.

The news media appear to be incapable of thinking about more than two hot spots at a time. Coverage of the so-called axis of evil—beyond parenthetical references—is no exception. Limited newsroom resources deserve part of the blame, as does the media's tendency to follow the political agenda set by the White House or dictated by the travels of the secretary of state. It is remarkable that the festering "clear and present danger" of an out-of-control nuclear weapons program in a desperate and irrational Stalinist nation—which already has the bomb—is sometimes not considered sexy enough for a headline.

The six-party negotiations over nuclear disbarment are finally bearing some kind of fruit. The tentative agreement involves a brittle step-by-step process that could go in circles, or fail, or even lead to a resolution of this final vestige of the Cold War. But how did we get from there to here? When Pyongyang is not screaming for attention with nuclear tests and missile launches, the hypothetical menace of Iranian missiles striking Israel continues to dominate the nuclear disarmament story. North Korea's stash of plutonium endangers the security of Northeast Asia—the locus of a phenomenally important chunk of the global economy—but that cannot compete, it seems, with the politics of oil. North Korea, then, remains a flash-in-the-pan hot spot.

The hot-spot phenomenon is important because it leaves readers and broadcast audiences with a narrow and momentary understanding of the world they live in. It also greatly inhibits the role of any journalist who seeks to capture the deeper meaning of events and write an accurate rough draft that historians can later redefine and revise. In many cases, hot-spot journalism reduces the foreign correspondent from being an informed observer with the capacity to integrate and interpret information to serving as a mere scribe and content provider. But it is unfair to blame the news consumer for having a short attention span, just as it is unfair to blame the messenger for delivering the message.

South Korea's Nelson Mandela

Consider the coverage of South Korea's iconic politician, former president Kim Dae-jung, someone who unquestionably will leave a lasting footprint on history as a heroic underdog, a political maverick, and a visionary statesman. Kim won the Nobel Peace Prize for his ice-breaking "sunshine policy" toward North Korea. Yet he was ostracized by the Bush administration, which believed his pragmatic diplomacy undermined its dogma of hard-line confrontation with North Korea. The post–September 11 press corps did little to burnish Kim's image.

Whether you like him or not, Kim is the living symbol of South Korea's defiant struggle against military dictatorship, having survived a government assassination plot, repeated imprisonment, and a death sentence for sedition. Despite his unpopularity today with many South Koreans outside his native Cholla Province, the Nobel laureate will likely be remembered more kindly in the future, along with the likes of Nelson Mandela, as a champion of human rights and human dignity. In a 2002 meeting with foreign journalists in Seoul, the frail octogenarian spoke lucidly and in detail about the North Korean nuclear problem, stressing the importance of patience and economic engagement instead of confrontation, a point of view that appears to be prevailing.[2]

What kind of foreign news coverage did Kim receive in December 1987 when he lost his quixotic bid for the presidency after Chun's capitulation? How did that coverage compare with the reporting in December 1997, when he was elected by a narrow margin as president of the government that once persecuted and tried to kill him? According to ProQuest, an information database that includes newspaper archives, coverage in the *New York Times* roughly reflected the fickleness of the hot-spot syndrome. For ten days before and after the December 17, 1987, election (when Kim was defeated), the newspaper published twenty bylined articles with a Seoul dateline citing Kim's name. In a comparable period in 1997, when he was elected head of a government that once tried to kill him, the number dropped to eleven articles. At least two highly reputable *New York Times* staff correspondents were on the ground in each case, but the intensity of the spotlight had faded by 1997, and the number of stories making it into print was nearly halved from the previous decade.

Was the amount of ink used in 1987 out of proportion to what the story merited? Was the number of stories published in 1997 entirely appropriate to the occasion, sufficient to inform readers and historians of the gravity of the event? No doubt other factors were at play—such as competition for space from other international news stories or the size of the news hole that determines coverage on a particular day. Financial reporting on the Asian economic crisis was gathering momentum by 1997 and competed with political news for attention.

Gi-Wook Shin's research study analyzing U.S. media coverage of Korean news, summarized in chapter 1 of this book, sheds light on the situation. Shin and his colleagues found that the number of words written about Korea's economy in the *New York Times* approximately tripled from 1987 and 1996, when they were roughly the same, to 1997, compared with the previous year and with 1987. By the same measure and in the same newspaper, the number of words about domestic politics declined by nearly 80 percent from the spike in 1987 to 1997. In 1997 economic stories were three times as prevalent as political stories, whereas in 1987, political stories appeared five times as frequently as articles about Korea's economy.[3]

It is important to record the level of political stability in South Korea at the time of these snapshots of news coverage. By 1997, when Kim's moment arrived, Korean democracy had matured to such a degree that fair elections and the peaceful transfer of power among leaders were taken for granted. Ten years earlier, this was not the case. In 1987 Korea witnessed a chaotic presidential election in which it was conceivable that tanks would roll if Roh Tae-woo, the candidate handpicked by strongman Chun, lost to a despised political dissident. The news media, when they are paying attention, exercise reasonably good judgment in identifying a given story's significance, but their agenda can be arbitrary and their vision unduly influenced by the high drama associated with a global hot spot.

Has the international press lost interest in monitoring the progress of South Korea's democratization since the hot-spot coverage of the late 1980s? I sought to understand this potential trend in June 2007 when I was preparing a paper for a journalism seminar hosted by the Korean Democracy Foundation in Seoul. A broad search of the ProQuest and Lexis-Nexis databases using such keywords as "South Korea" and "democracy" yielded deceptive results. Redundancy made analysis difficult—news service articles republished in several newspapers get multiple citations, as do stories that reappear in different editions of the same newspaper. However, I did uncover revealing data using a narrow search for articles that mentioned South Korea's draconian National Security Act of 1947 (NSA). There were numerous results for the late 1980s, when many journalists covered the human rights violations perpetrated under the guise of this law. But in subsequent years there was hardly a mention of the NSA. Based on news archives alone, it was impossible to learn whether the law had been abolished or reformed, as promised twenty years previously. In fact, legal experts I consulted confirmed that the law, which was created to protect South Koreans from the North Korean threat, remains on the books without major revisions. It still gives the government the power to crack down at whim on antistate political dissent, and its survival—even in its amended form—could represent a latent threat to democracy and human rights. Significantly, that crucial point has been either lost or understated in this phase of foreign news coverage of South Korea.[4]

Lost in Translation

How do the news media function today, as opposed to in the late 1980s, and how do changing values in news judgment apply to coverage of South Korea? Today's hot spots are covered differently than they were twenty years ago because contemporary news organizations face declining advertising revenues and lower profit margins. The trend of consolidating media properties within corporate chains focused on quarterly financial results has also profoundly affected the way news organizations report the news and deploy their resources. Foreign news is now a luxury, not a necessity, and business news has increased at the expense of general news. Coverage of salacious crime and celebrity imbroglios is also on the rise.

Foreign news coverage is no longer deemed an important contributor to the quality of the "product," whose purpose is to entertain and retain readers. Accordingly, foreign bureaus are being drastically reduced and, in many cases, eliminated. For example, the Knight Ridder chain (now McClatchy) has closed its bureau in Tokyo and now covers the Koreas out of Beijing. The *Los Angeles Times* maintains a traditional interest in the Korean Peninsula and Northeast Asia because of its large Asian ethnic readership and the city's position as an economic hub on the Pacific Rim. Nevertheless, it has reduced its staff in Tokyo from three journalists with area expertise and advanced language skills to a single itinerant correspondent who works from home because his bureau has been closed. To its credit, the paper more recently based a staff reporter in Seoul for several years, but it did not replace her when she left. Like many other newspapers, the *Los Angeles Times* faces a crisis of newsroom layoffs and a deterioration of its core mission to cover global news with authority and integrity.

Under these reduced circumstances, foreign journalism has changed considerably, and for the worse. More than ever before, the remaining correspondents based in foreign bureaus rotate in and out of hot spots. They have no time to engage in serious language study or to accumulate deep local knowledge of the countries in which they are based. Former correspondents who could offer their expertise are a dying breed, as they are particularly susceptible to buyouts and layoffs because of their age and high salaries. Coverage of China is a notable exception to this trend: the vast nation is one big hot spot, and Chinese economic news is crucial for the high-income readers of the business section on whom advertisers dote. Consequently, major newspapers maintain bureaus in Beijing, including seasoned correspondents with advanced knowledge of the country and fluency in Chinese. Overall, however, the picture is bleak, and ignorance about places like South Korea, both in the press corps and in the public, is on the rise. American journalism is failing to cover the whole world.

Americans Love to Be Hated

Declining standards in journalism have contributed to the blowback of anti-Americanism, in Korea as well as in Iraq and elsewhere in the Middle East. Foreign correspondents have always been frustrated by the tendency of their home offices to second-guess their news judgments, but when their local knowledge is no longer relevant, the problem is compounded. The consumers of the news may not notice this deficiency, but subjects of news coverage do, and they are increasingly aware of how they are portrayed as their stories flash back at them through global media outlets such as CNN and Al Jazeera.

In South Korea, people have long had unfettered access to the television channel that broadcasts the U.S. military's Far Eastern Network (FEN). Though the FEN is meant to be an amenity for locally stationed troops, anyone can tune in to the station to access U.S. network news, warts and all. Given that CNN cable feeds and even Japanese broadcasts were not available to ordinary South Koreans until recently, many South Koreans relied on the FEN for information and entertainment. Yet some Koreans were deeply offended by the stereotypical manner in which they were portrayed on the popular sitcom *M*A*S*H*, which was set during the not-so-funny Korean War. In the critical period of the late 1980s especially, the distorted hot-spot characterization of Koreans as violent people grated on the nerves of the FEN's unintended audience. During the Seoul Olympic Games, too, many FEN viewers were irritated by the network's over-the-top patriotic coverage of American athletes and lack of attention to contenders from their host nation. When irate Korean boxing fans threw chairs at a referee who made a controversial call during a fight, the image was broadcast repeatedly for days, as if it were a statement on the Korean national character.

The notion that Koreans might be more sensitive to criticism than other nationalities, and therefore react disproportionately, is of course nonsense—an artifact of cultural preconceptions that sloppy journalism can sometimes fall prey to. In hot-spot journalism, such misperceptions can run amok and then reinforce themselves. In the case of South Korea, unfavorable images of Koreans boomeranged back in their faces, cutting deep and exacerbating feelings of anti-Americanism. American journalists based in Seoul and elsewhere in the region were left to pick up the pieces and explain the underpinnings of the problem.

Anti-American blowback is a complex matter, and as observers around the world will attest, it is often based on legitimate grievances and reflects conflicted feelings. Most people make the important distinction between the U.S. government, which they may despise, and the American people, whom they generally admire. This distinction can be obscured when crowd psychology takes over, though. In South Korea, the older generation harbors deep gratitude for the sacrifices Americans made to protect their freedom during the Korean War. But the vocal younger generation does not share this sentiment and is likely to be indignant about the duplicity of U.S. Cold War policy.[5]

Allegations that the United States may have been complicit, by dint of a hands-off policy, in the 1980 Kwangju massacre fueled mistrust. So did the overwhelming presence of American troops stationed in the heart of Seoul and the U.S. government's foot-dragging on promises to move the sprawling Yongsan Army Garrison to a less populated area. The Yongsan base made many South Koreans feel that their country was under military occupation. Crimes by U.S. soldiers and road accidents ignited protests. The creeping invasion of popular culture from the United States provoked nationalistic resistance in South Korea, as it has around the world.

The key point about covering anti-Americanism is that news editors cannot get enough of it. Their appetite for denunciations of the Great Satan appears limitless, because anti-Americanism appeals to a delicious sense of indignation among U.S. media consumers. Many Americans are mystified by the ingratitude of people who hate the United States, which they view as a generous and altruistic nation that spreads democracy and defends the free world with its military might. Americans' failure to move beyond this simplistic mind-set is spawning tragic results among Muslim populations today, and remains a problem on the Korean Peninsula. But many of the information gatekeepers in the newsroom who propagate such thinking are uninterested in changing their approach. Indeed, most editors believe that people want to be told what they already know, as opposed to learning something that might challenge their comfortable preconceived ideas. Accordingly, many correspondents covering South Korea have received "rockets" from their editors, urgent alerts that a competitor had a story about anti-Americanism, whether spouted by student demonstrators or posited by a political science professor. To be sure, in the heat of the moment, angry crowds of Korean protesters occasionally threatened American journalists, but this was the exception, not the rule. Expressions of anti-Americanism in South Korea became so commonplace and formulaic that they lost their significance to the jaded reporters who covered them. This enervation notwithstanding, the story about the latest anti-American diatribe had to be matched, feeding into an echo chamber that perpetuates half-truths and glib impressions.

The Gift of Poetry

Before traveling to Seoul in 2007 for the Korean Democracy Foundation's journalism seminar, I reexamined electronic clippings of my old stories on South Korea. As a Japan reporter, I never felt especially competent in my reporting in Seoul, but I came across one article that resonated with me as much as when I had first written it. It was about Koreans' passion for poetry. It was written at the end of 1988 after the excitement of the Olympic Games had faded and South Koreans were beginning to poke fun at their fallen dictator, Chun Doo-hwan, instead of screaming about his misdeeds. The hot spot's klieg lights had dimmed; it was now time to relax and reflect.

The headline was "Irish of Asia: South Koreans Just Love to Wax Lyrical." The story's lead described a live radio broadcast in which the host challenged random passersby at a downtown Seoul street corner to compose a poem on the spot about the corruption and injustice of Chun's reign. Nor could it be just any poem—it had to have four lines, and the first word of each line had to begin with one of the syllables from the Korean vernacular for Fifth Republic corruption—O-Kong-Pi-Ri—in that order. Incredibly, almost all of the impromptu poets passed the test, my trusted interpreter and local informant told me, as we listened to the broadcast while riding in a taxicab. One poet mustered a ditty that compared Chun's balding pate to a moon shining over the neighborhood where he lived under house arrest.[6]

I was inspired to dig deeper and to learn more about this extraordinary capacity for verse. It turned out to be a kind of national trait, entirely at odds with the hackneyed rough-edged image of the Korean everyman. As I wrote admiringly in the article:

> Serious poems are printed on chewing gum wrappers, scrawled on graffiti-covered walls, mounted in frames in the subway, published in newspapers and recited with much aspiration in coffee shops and theaters. Anyone needing a quick poetry fix can call a dial-a-poem telephone number. . . .
>
> Poets are heroes. They may not get rich at it, but the vocation does not carry any of the stigma of eccentricity it might in the West. Korean history is populated by scholar-statesmen for whom proficiency in Chinese verse was a decisive subject in civil service examinations. Today, nearly everyone will confess to having written a poem at one time, usually in student days, to express private feelings.[7]

I wish I had possessed the leisure to write more stories like this during the noisy year that preceded its publication, stories that get into the hearts of the people we journalists cover, rather than casting them in a boilerplate political docudrama. I would like to believe that in calmer, saner times, foreign journalists have come to Korea and written stories illuminating the spirit of an extraordinary people, and that others will continue to do so in the future.

Notes

[1] Kofi Annan, foreword, *The Media and the Rwanda Genocide*, ed. Allen Thompson (London: International Development Research Center and Pluto Press, 2007), 3.

[2] Karl Schoenberger, "Scandal Tarnishes Kim's Legacy: South Korean Leader's 'Sunshine Policy' toward North Threatened," *San Jose Mercury News*, May 12, 2002.

[3] See Gi-Wook Shin, *One Alliance, Two Lenses: U.S.-Korea Relations in a New Era* (Stanford, CA: Stanford University Press, 2009).

[4] Karl Schoenberger, "Korea's Struggle for Human Rights: The Path from Dictatorship to Democracy" (paper presented to the Korea Democracy Foundation, Seoul, June 8, 2007); Amnesty International, "Open Letter to All Leaders of Political Parties: An Important Duty to Revitalize Efforts to Fundamentally Repeal or Review the National Security Law" (AI Doc. 25/009/2004), October 13, 2004; and author's personal communication with Kun Yang, law professor at Hanyang University's College Law, May 18, 2007.

[5] Mark L. Clifford, *Troubled Tiger: Businessmen, Bureaucrats, and Generals in South Korea* (Armonk, NY: M.E. Sharpe, 1994).

[6] Karl Schoenberger, "The Irish of Asia: South Koreans Just Love to Wax Lyrical," *Los Angeles Times*, December 16, 1988, 1.

[7] Ibid.

COVERING KOREA IN THE 1980S: THE DEMOCRACY STORY

Daniel C. Sneider

In the summer of 1986, less than a year after coming to Tokyo to report for the *Christian Science Monitor*, I made my first reporting trip to South Korea. The story I wrote began, in customary fashion, with an anecdote. It recounted the dilemma of a professor, a department chairman at a prestigious university, whose students had been discovered storing the makings of Molotov cocktails in the department's offices, preparing for confrontations with police. Should the students be turned in to the authorities? The professor opted instead for dialogue. "If I turn them in," he told me, "then we would lose all possibility of being able to talk to these students."[1]

My story depicted Korea as a society torn between two extremes—a radical student movement no longer bound by the ideological taboos of the Korean War versus young, hard-line military officers, men who saw even the military-led government of General Chun Doo-hwan as too weak. In between was a growing Korean middle class, eager for democratic change but wary of extremists.

One important factor in this volatile mix, I suggested, was the increasing unease of the United States, always an outsize player in South Korea's internal dynamics. Behind the scenes, U.S. officials were pushing the Chun regime to liberalize before things got out of control. "The next months," my story ended, "will be a crucial test of the ability of middle-of-the-road South Koreans to make this attempt at true political participation succeed."

Less than a year later, in June 1987, I found myself in the streets of Seoul, an army surplus gas mask pulled over my head, witnessing pitched battles between students hurling rocks and firebombs and heavily armored paramilitary riot police responding with volleys of powerful pepper gas. At times, the center of Seoul seemed like one large battleground as police chased protesters down the streets and alleys to prevent any significant gatherings of demonstrators.

For a few crucial days in late June, South Korea stood perilously on the edge of political disaster. The student movement had managed to burst beyond the boundaries of the campus, drawing ordinary Koreans into its ranks, from middle-class churchgoers to industrial workers. The Chun regime was desperately trying to stay in power. Quietly, but increasingly publicly, the Reagan administration was sending the message that Chun needed to step aside, as he had promised to do when he seized power at the beginning of the decade. But some in the Korean military, including Chun himself, believed this would lead to a takeover by their longtime foe, dissident leader Kim Dae-jung, viewed by some in the army as a Communist.

At one point, I was told by one of my best sources—an American political adviser to the U.S. Forces in Korea (USFK) who was deeply familiar with the inner workings of the South Korean military—that "the tank engines were warming up," a colorful metaphor for an imminent coup d'état. As I reported at the time, Chun had met secretly with senior army commanders and secured their pledge to impose martial law.

Chun backed off at the last minute. The mass uprising shook support for the regime from within its own elite, who worried that South Korea's emergence as an economic power—a position soon to be celebrated by hosting the 1988 Olympics—was in jeopardy. But there was also a crucial intervention by the U.S. ambassador, Jim Lilley, a tough-talking former CIA official, accompanied by Assistant Secretary of State Gaston Sigur, a former academic, who delivered a private warning that the United States would oppose any attempt to impose emergency rule.

The events that followed this dramatic confrontation moved with amazing speed. By December 1987, South Korea held its first truly free presidential election, followed some months later by parliamentary elections. The December election was memorable. I witnessed truly massive political rallies, numbering sometimes half a million or more people. These seas of Koreans, gathered in Pusan's dusty fields or Seoul's concrete plazas, sought to assert their newfound democratic rights as much as to support a particular candidate. South Korea remained in the midst of turmoil for much of this time—student protests continued, and radicals moved, often in underground fashion, into the ranks of labor, organizing unions to challenge Korea's biggest corporate conglomerates.

Covering South Korea's democratic revolution remains one of the highlights of my journalistic career. It is a rare privilege for a correspondent to bear witness to that kind of historic change. It was also remarkable in two other respects. First, perhaps for the first time since the Korean War, a story out of the Korean Peninsula dominated the front pages of American newspapers for almost a month. In part that was a product of serendipity—it was a slow news time, as summer months can sometimes be, and there was no other major story competing for column inches and for the attention of readers and editors.

Second, the story was almost entirely about South Korea itself; Koreans were the main actors, with Americans playing an important but secondary role. Previously (and since), American media coverage of Korea tended to follow the agenda of Washington policymakers. South Korea was seen as a Cold War battlefield in an ongoing story whose main actors were the nearly forty thousand American troops stationed along the heavily militarized frontier with Communist North Korea. Certainly, human rights and struggles for democracy formed a part of the media narrative in the 1970s, but almost always in the context of confrontations with the North Korean regime.

Media coverage in the 1980s, on the other hand, was shaped almost entirely by the tale of democratic transformation. To be sure, security issues were a constant—even in these years—from startling acts of North Korean terrorism early in the decade to the beginnings of the nuclear crisis at its close. And South Korea's emergence as a major player in the world economy (and a partner to the United States) also attracted attention. But overall, the 1980s were a time of democratization. And the tale that the U.S. media told was a tale of the Korean people themselves, marking the first time that Koreans took center stage in the American consciousness.

In political terms, the narrative of this period began with the assassination of Park Chung-hee in October 1979, followed by the seizure of power by Chun and his military allies. What we now understand as the defining moment for all that followed was the bloody massacre of antigovernment protesters in Kwangju in May 1980, an event that still shapes South Korean politics and influences perceptions of the United States. The unrest continued with the arrest of dissident leader Kim Dae-jung and his planned execution, averted only through American intervention. Political unease, fomented by students, began to increase from the middle of the decade.

It was during this time that I came to Tokyo as a correspondent for the *Christian Science Monitor*, covering both Japan and Korea. I arrived in 1985 and was later joined by my senior colleague Takashi Oka, who was my mentor in many respects, not least regarding South Korea. Takashi was a veteran reporter in this part of the globe, not only for the *Monitor* but also, earlier, for the *New York Times*, and he had covered South Korea during the first few years of the 1980s. Between the two of us, we produced most of the coverage of the Korean Peninsula during the decade, supplemented in the mid-1980s by the work of some excellent stringers in Seoul, notably Steve Butler, who also reported for the *Financial Times*. (Oka and I also performed duties for the *Monitor*'s other media—he for Monitor Television and I for Monitor Radio.)

A survey of the *Monitor*'s coverage of South Korea over the 1980s, including stories generated by other bureaus, especially the Washington bureau, bears out my impressions of our coverage focus. The survey divided the coverage into four main subject areas: South Korea, North Korea, the economy, and U.S.-ROK relations. Other stories relevant to South Korea—such as those dealing with North-South relations—were included in the latter three categories. Stories focused on South Korea were heavily concerned with domestic politics and, to a lesser extent, with Korean culture and society.

As figure 3.1 makes clear, stories about South Korea dominated the *Christian Science Monitor*'s coverage of the Korean Peninsula during the 1980s, accounting for about two-thirds of the stories written. Stories about the economy and about North Korea ran in roughly equivalent numbers, with the U.S.-ROK alliance coming in a distant fourth in the paper's coverage priorities. Coverage of South Korea jumped dramatically between 1987 and 1988, again reflecting the democracy story. We filed some seventy-nine bylined stories about the Korean

Peninsula in 1987—a remarkable number considering that the *Monitor* had no weekend editions (like the *Wall Street Journal* until recently), meaning that the Koreas appeared in more than one out of every four editions of the paper.

Figure 3.1 U.S. Media Coverage of the Korean Peninsula: The *Christian Science Monitor*, 1980–1989

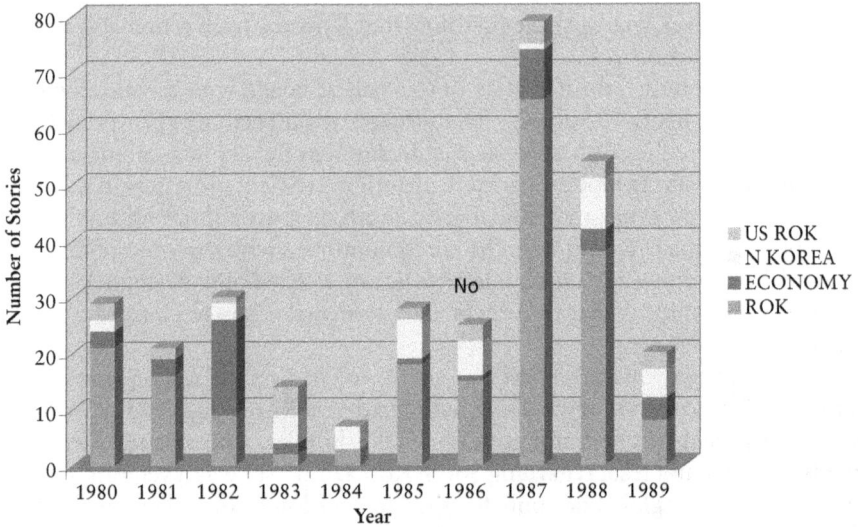

Note: ROK = South Korea; US ROK = U.S.-ROK relations.

Almost without exception, correspondents decided which stories to cover. This was particularly true with regard to foreign news—the *Monitor* prided itself on having a core group of experienced foreign correspondents, and foreign coverage was one of its strengths. Of course we journalists did consult with our editors, and they decided where and when a story ran in the paper.

Though I do not have the data comparing Korean coverage across U.S. newspapers during the 1980s, judging from what my colleagues at other papers were writing at the time, I do not think the *Monitor* was significantly out of sync with the competition. But it may have been unusual in two respects: First, the *Monitor* was a national, even an international newspaper, in which foreign news was the prominent element of its overall coverage. Second, unlike most U.S. papers—or Japanese ones, for that matter—the *Monitor* did not require its writers to explain how a foreign news story impacted readers at home, nor did it privilege stories with an obvious U.S. link over those without one. Its editors believed that explaining events in other countries to U.S. readers had intrinsic value.

Sources of Coverage

For American reporters, South Korea in the 1980s had two dominant features, apparently contradictory but coexistent, that shaped how we went about covering the country.

On the one hand, it was still an authoritarian state in which the security services, operating under the draconian National Security Law, enjoyed considerable power. These institutions, and their role in South Korean society and politics, persisted well beyond the democratic uprising of 1987. Even though he came to power via democratic means, the election of Roh Tae-woo—Chun's longtime, though more moderate, military partner—created considerable ambiguity about the future of democratic rule. I frequently engaged with sources—particularly radical students, labor organizers, and human rights activists—who operated either underground or in fear of government repression. As I will explain, I spent a great deal of time cultivating these sources and was often concerned about protecting their identities so they would talk to me about what was, at that time, usually illegal activity. Most American reporters assumed that the South Korean security services—the Korean Central Intelligence Agency and its successor organizations—monitored our activities. Many took it as a given that our hotel rooms were bugged and our telephones were tapped.

Yet on the other hand, American reporters enjoyed extraordinary access at all levels of South Korean society, particularly within the nation's political and governmental structures. This was in part a product of the United States' broad and deep influence and power in South Korea, symbolized by the large American military contingent, whose presence was felt on a daily basis in Seoul. The American media were in some ways treated as an extension of the apparatus of American power. Korean officials were very sophisticated in their understanding of how the media could be used to shape the messages they sought to convey to Washington. Conversely, they were fearful of how negative coverage might affect their fate.

The Korean Overseas Information Service (KOIS), the information arm of the South Korean government, was a powerful agency in those days, one that could provide—or deny—access to the highest levels of the government. I enjoyed a good working relationship with its directors, as did other American correspondents, though I did not depend on KOIS for access.

My *Monitor* colleague Oka and I met regularly with senior Korean government officials, not only those in the Foreign Ministry but also prominent members of the Cabinet. More important, during the democratic changes of the late 1980s, we were able to spend considerable time with the leaders of the opposition—the so-called Three Kims: Kim Dae-jung, Kim Young-sam, and Kim Jong-pil. At key moments, they were usually available, sometimes by phone, sometimes face to face, to give us their views. Kim Dae-jung's kitchen table, particularly when he was still under house arrest, was a familiar place to some correspondents, whose accounts were often his only way to communicate to the world, including to Koreans. For American journalists, such meetings were crucial to understanding the individuals who shaped this period of South Korea's development.

I also made use of the American establishment in Korea, both as a valuable source of background information and, at times, as a sounding board to gauge my impressions of current developments. As a matter of course, I developed sources at the U.S. Embassy in Seoul. Its squat, ugly building sat across the boulevard from the main offices of the South Korean ministries and was almost an unofficial second government, with American ambassadors and senior embassy officials participating in the unfolding political events. Ambassadors Richard "Dixie" Walker, Jim Lilley, and Donald Gregg all served while I was a reporter in the country, and I came to respect them as insightful representatives of the United States. These men—and with few exceptions in those days all the ambassadors were men—were almost all professionals either of the Foreign Service or the intelligence community, and were well versed in Korean life. Washington gave them considerable leeway to act, something that is rarely true today. The United States military command was in some sense a separate, and sometimes rival, center of power to the U.S. Embassy, but it, too, served as a source of information, particularly concerning the Korean military, with which the USFK maintained very close ties.

It is important here to mention a personal aspect of my use and access to sources in the South Korean leadership and the U.S. establishment. My father, the late Richard L. Sneider, was the U.S. ambassador to Korea from 1974 to 1978. He was still alive when I began reporting from Seoul, and he had remained active in U.S.-Korean relations after his retirement. My name opened many doors for me in South Korea, for which I was always grateful.

Origins of the 386 Generation

While I spent considerable time with politicians and officials, my de facto second office in Korea was located well away from the corridors of official power—it was on the campus of Yonsei University, one of Korea's elite private institutions. Yonsei was the unofficial headquarters of the South Korean student movement. Meetings of student organizations from around the country took place there, and it was the site of almost daily clashes with the helmeted, shielded, riot police that stood on constant guard outside the university's main gate to block demonstrators from leaving. The railroad embankment opposite the main gate offered the best perch for photographers and reporters to watch the action. It was jokingly referred to as "going to the beach," and journalists proudly claimed membership in the Yonsei Beach Club. The Seoul Foreign Correspondents Club even had shirts made for the "club," depicting a reporter wearing one of the uncomfortable gas masks we all carried around with us.

I spent most of my time inside the gates, however, meeting with ordinary students and student leaders at the offices of the student newspaper, the *Yonsei*

Annals, and the student campus organization. Yonsei was always my first stop after arriving in Seoul—a practice I took up again when I returned to cover South Korea in the early 2000s for the *San Jose Mercury News*. At Yonsei I also benefited from the insight and wisdom of Dr. Horace Underwood, an American scholar and Yonsei administrator who had lived in Korea for more than a half century.

My talks with students led me in turn to more underground groups of student radicals, some of whom had left the campus to become labor organizers, others who had become part of Marxist movements, and still others who had embraced the forbidden ideology of the North Korean regime. The activity of all these groups was illegal under the National Security Law.

One of the last *Monitor* stories I filed from South Korea, in October 1989, began with a clandestine meeting with a twenty-one-year-old student from Dongguk University who was hiding from security police. He was being sought for his role in organizing a campus performance of *Sea of Blood*, a stock North Korean drama. Some twenty-five hundred riot police had stormed the stage twenty minutes into the opening act, firing tear gas and stripping the stage of props and equipment, while battling radical students. My story explored the allure of the North, an appeal largely bolstered by its status as the forbidden fruit. I also considered the North's continuing image as a purer, more traditional society, unadulterated by American popular culture. I recounted a story told to me by an old friend, Professor Lee In-ho, who taught courses on Russian history and Communism, and later became the Korean ambassador to Moscow. When she taught in the early 1980s, Dr. Lee was unable to discuss the writings of Marx and Engels for fear that her students would be punished for having textbooks that referred to these writings, even if only to criticize them. Meanwhile, Marxist tracts were circulating widely through underground networks. By the time the government eased restrictions on teaching the material, "it was too late to compete," she told me.

Anti-American rhetoric was intense among these students, and I wrote about this subject frequently, as did Takashi Oka. We saw that such views were a product of a deeper antipathy to the South Korean authoritarian regime, which was widely perceived as being propped up—if not controlled—by the United States. Even after Americans played a key role in bringing down Chun, these beliefs remained so deeply embedded that little could alter them.

The memories of these times came back to me more recently when I returned to reporting in Korea after the 2002 election that brought former labor lawyer and human rights activist Roh Moo-hyun to the Korean presidency. Along with Roh came a new generation of the power elite—what the Korean press calls the "386 generation." This is shorthand for those whom I watched march out of Yonsei University, only to be met by the police, and who rallied outside the gates of Hyundai shipyards, exhorting workers to join unions—the generation of South Koreans who were in their thirties, had attended university in the 1980s, and were born in the 1960s.

I later interviewed some of the 386ers who came to power in Seoul. For example, I profiled Im Jong-sok: he is an impressive member of the National Assembly, a former student radical who had been imprisoned for activities such as climbing over the wall of the U.S. ambassador's residence. Assemblyman Im and I have traded tales from that era and have discussed numerous other sensitive topics, from U.S. policy in Iraq to North Korea's nuclear program. Because I understood South Korea's democratic transformation, I was able to see beyond his initial anti-American rhetoric.

Ironically, while Koreans focus intently on their relationship with the United States—a country that has, after all, made countless decisions determining the peninsula's destiny—Americans' interest in and awareness of Koreans have been fleeting. From the decision to divide Korea into American and Soviet zones of occupation at the close of the war to the response to the North Korean invasion in 1950, American policymakers have historically given very little thought to Koreans themselves. Instead, questions of geopolitics have dominated American calculations, Korea being merely one battlefield in a much broader conflict.

The U.S. media have tended to follow this same pattern, paying attention to the region when it fits into larger issues of American foreign policy, but otherwise usually ignoring what goes on there. The long-term Cold War deployment of American troops on the peninsula after the Korean armistice shaped not only policy but also perception. In American eyes, Korea was, and for the most part remains, a security problem and a security story. But the cost of this limited policy and press focus is that we sometimes fail to understand the region and its people. Consequently, we overlook small developments that lurk beneath the surface until they emerge to reshape history. In South Korea, this has been true for some time. And it may be also true today in North Korea, where the U.S. media's fixation on the nuclear weapons program obscures the vast social changes going on within that totalitarian black box.

Note

[1] Daniel C. Sneider, "S. Korea's Uneasy Extremes," *Christian Science Monitor*, July 11, 1986.

DEMOCRACY, ANTI-AMERICANISM, AND KOREAN NATIONALISM

Doug Struck

O n a cold December evening in 2002, Sister Lucia came out with the other nuns from the Sisters of the Korean Martyrs Catholic convent in Seoul to hold a candle in a crowd. On the lapel of her coat, over her religious habit, was a pin. It read: "F—— USA."

"Yankee, go home!" she chanted, arm raised toward the stiff line of riot police guarding the U.S. Embassy.

The September 11, 2001, attacks in New York and Washington had prompted the world to rally to the side of the United States in an outpouring of sympathy for Americans. But now, barely fifteen months later, South Korea was gripped in a frenzy of anti-Americanism and fervent nationalism.

Thousands of demonstrators took to the streets, blowing whistles, carrying candles, and denouncing the American presence. Protesters camped outside the U.S. military headquarters in Seoul, broadcasting profanities through loudspeakers. About fifty protesters cut the fence and stormed an American base near Seoul on November 26; others threw gasoline bombs into a second base. American pedestrians were roughed up, a U.S. congressional tour was canceled for safety, and U.S. commanders confined soldiers to their bases to keep them off the streets.

The demonstrators included students and leftists long opposed to the U.S. troop presence in South Korea. But they were joined by nuns such as Sister Lucia, Buddhist monks, pop stars, teachers, movie idols, and citizens who normally would not have been seen on picket lines. The movement appeared to have grave potential. "This anti-Americanism is hurting our national interest," President Kim Dae-jung warned the protesters.

The U.S. media did not ignore these events. As detailed in chapter 1, there was an upsurge of newspaper articles on the Koreas at the time. But in most cases, we who covered North and South Korea treated the stories coming out of those countries as separate and distinct subjects. For example, we wrote the story of the South Korean election as if it were just another episode in the country's still nascent democracy. We wrote the anti-Americanism story as if it were a discrete event. And we wrote the North Korean story as if it were isolated from the other issues. In fact, these issues were intertwined, and each reverberated in the others. I would suggest that the chief deficiency of U.S. coverage of the peninsula during that period was that we reporters did not paint a broad enough portrait of the events as they unfolded.

The December 2002 protests offer a case in point. They took place in the midst of a sharp and ominous upsurge of resentment toward the United States, which seemed more than a passing phase. One diplomat, a longtime Korea watcher, described the demonstrations as "the most dramatic events involving the U.S. troops here in fifty years."

The focal point of these protests was a tragic accident on June 13, 2002, and the subsequent manner in which U.S. authorities seemed—to South Koreans—to brush off responsibility for it. On that day, a U.S. Army infantry division moved huge armored mine-clearing vehicles from their base to training grounds outside Seoul. The soldiers took a road too narrow for the big vehicles and rounded a blind curve too fast. Two schoolgirls, Shim Mi-son and Shin Hyo-sun, both fourteen, were walking on the pedestrian shoulder of the road, and both were crushed under the wheels of one of the machines.

Because the accident happened while they were on duty, the driver, Sgt. Mark Walker, and the commander of the vehicle, Sgt. Fernando Nino, were charged in a U.S. military court instead of a South Korean civilian court. After separate trials, on November 20 and 23, 2002, the military court found both men not guilty on charges of negligent homicide. They were quickly transferred out of the country.

The public reacted with fury. Critics called the process a sham, "a trial of an accomplice by accomplices." Protests erupted, demanding justice for the "murders" of the girls. Photographs of what was left of the girls' bodies further inflamed public emotions. The grim pictures, which no newspapers consented to print, quickly spread on the Internet.

"Anti-American sentiments have spread into almost all strata of Korean society," reported Kim Seung-Hwan in the Korea Times.

Cultural differences also played a role. Had the South Korean military been involved—or the military of many other Asian nations, for that matter—such an incident would have prompted the officer in charge to resign immediately or a top political figure to take responsibility. No American officer resigned. No one was publicly punished. The U.S. Army even refused to say whether administrative action was taken, citing the privacy of its soldiers. South Koreans angrily dismissed a belated statement of regret by President George W. Bush—read not by him but by the U.S. ambassador to South Korea—as weak, late, and insincere.

Most U.S. news stories concentrated on the military accident as the cause of the demonstrations, with occasional brief mention of other events swirling around at the time. To identify this focus is not to indict American reporting on these events but merely to describe the content of the resulting journalism. Newspaper reporting is much like our own sense of sight: we can inspect something closely or we can take a broad view of a great landscape, but no matter how much we adjust our field of vision, we cannot see everything at once. Likewise, we reporters try to put the events we cover into a larger context, to provide the texture of the times; but we cannot offer up the whole sweep of history, the complex backdrop against which certain events play out. Instead, we simplify, we categorize, and sometimes we generalize. These are useful methods for trying to grasp new, difficult, or alien concepts—to sort events from the static of life—and most people, whether reporters or not, employ them. Such sorting is the very process of "seeing." So it is that I affirm, without apology, that the stories—my stories—about the demonstrations in South Korea offered up only a thin slice of the fuller explanation for those events.

Any one of a number of starting points, including Kim Dae-jung's election, would have provided a more complete view of South Korea's turmoil during this period. However, for my analysis, June 13, 2000, is a useful beginning. On that day, Kim Dae-jung motored down a wide boulevard in Pyongyang lined with thousands of North Koreans in colorful traditional dress, brought out to cheer him. Kim Dae-jung sat beside North Korea's ruler, Kim Jong-il. It was the first meeting between the leaders of the two Koreas since the countries were separated more than fifty years earlier, in 1945.

In Seoul there was much cheering as well. South Koreans were transfixed by the event, swelling with national and ethnic pride. South Koreans gathered in parks and huddled around televisions, watching the extraordinary live satellite broadcast of what many hoped was the prelude to reconciliation between the two countries. Some viewers cried; some clutched faded photos of family members on the other side of the armed border. Here, for the first time, Koreans had taken control of their own destiny and moved it in a positive direction.

But the euphoria of the meeting, followed by wrenchingly limited family reunions and new snags in negotiations, soon dissipated. With the inauguration of George W. Bush in January 2001, American caution over the new détente in the region became outright hostility. In his first meeting with Nobel Prize winner Kim Dae-jung, in March 2001, President Bush bluntly and publicly rebuked Kim's "sunshine policy" of reconciliation.

The insult—Bush's treatment of Kim was described as shabby—came only a few months after a U.S. Pentagon report absolved American soldiers in the Korean War of deliberately firing on fleeing civilians near the tiny village of No Gun Ri, a bloody incident carefully documented by the Associated Press a year earlier. Responding to the new American hard line and Bush's thumping missile defense promotion, North Korea ratcheted up its own missile threats and slowed contacts with South Korea. South Korea's pride in its new course of action took a beating.

U.S. reporters were writing about the stalled progress of Korean relations when the hijacked-plane attacks on the World Trade Center and the Pentagon diverted the world's attention. Bush, reinventing himself as a "war president," brought North Korea back into his figurative rifle sights in his State of the Union speech in January 2002 by inexplicably dubbing it part of an "axis of evil" with Iraq and Iran.

As news writers grappled with the fallout from Bush's words, South Koreans could only watch as their hopes for a new peace on the continent evaporated. Soon, their anger at Bush's heavy-handed rhetoric was redirected toward the thirty-seven thousand American military personnel stationed in South Korea, seven thousand of whom were located right in the heart of their capital city, Seoul. Irritation with the U.S. military presence had waxed and waned through the years, taking the form of heated protests in the 1980s. But now the American soldiers seemed to symbolize not only an insensitivity to South Korean nationalism but also a heightened American arrogance in world affairs.

In June 2002, South Korea and Japan cohosted a nearly flawless World Cup. Three months later, the North and South Korean teams appeared jointly under one flag at the September Asian Games in Busan. Both of these events bolstered South Korean feelings that they were better off without U.S. interference in their affairs. The mood was stoked by the South Korean presidential campaign, during which candidate Roh Moo-hyun—a rough-talking self-taught lawyer who had represented labor activists and student dissidents—offered up promises to change what he described as his country's subservient relationship to the United States.

He struck a popular chord. He criticized South Korean politicians for their traditional pilgrimage to the United States to get a "political blessing" from Washington. He condemned the "hard-line policies of Bush" under which the U.S. government had refused to talk to North Korea. The public mood even forced Roh's conservative opponent, Lee Hoi-chang, to criticize the American government, saying the stiff diplomatic apology for the death of the two girls crushed by the U.S. military vehicle had "humiliated" South Koreans—but Roh came out on top and won the election.

This swirl of events coalesced into the street demonstrations of December 2002. The protests were undoubtedly fueled by some South Korean media's inflammatory coverage of the events. The demonstrations did make front-page news in the United States, amid stories about increasing world anxiety over the North Korean nuclear threats and, to a lesser extent, the South Korean election. To tie the events together, however, would have required a deft analytical approach better left to academics and political experts. Most journalists did not venture there. Instead, we offered an explanation of the events that was, if not inaccurate, nevertheless incomplete.

Did we fail our readers by not reaching for the broader context of the demonstrations, by not explaining that they were the product of more than a tragic traffic accident? Without question, some of our stories made reference to those wider connections, often in the journalistic shorthand needed to keep stories at a readable length. But in hindsight, I believe we may have missed the mark.

Like Congress, the U.S. media were timid in challenging President Bush's expansion of the "war on terror" to Iraq. Such timidity may also have prevented us from candidly weighing the collateral damage of his hard-line policies on the Korean Peninsula. Perhaps our inability to decipher the ambivalence between North and South Korea—countries that are at once fervent brothers and passionate enemies—made us shy away from reporting the emotions behind the demonstrations. Perhaps we were too reluctant to concede that after fifty years, American troops in South Korea were no longer seen as protectors but rather as a burden to the national psyche. These were the shortcomings of our reporting at the time. The reporting was not wrong, but it failed to encompass enough of the emotional mix of the time.

The symbiosis of these currents was demonstrated just a few months later, in early 2003. The growing North Korean nuclear threat, the northern regime's unwillingness to make further advances under the sunshine policy, and U.S. defense secretary Donald Rumsfeld's suggestion that the U.S. troop contingent in South Korea be downsized all threw cold water on the heated public mood. The street demonstrations and open anti-Americanism abruptly stopped in March, as South Koreans paused to ponder a future with more uncertainties than they had expected.

Western reporters, who are often more at ease covering something that happens rather than something that doesn't, tentatively noted the drop in anti-Americanism. We registered the confluence of Rumsfeld's remarks and the dissipation of protests but offered little additional analysis. Had we understood more fully the mix of nationalism, pride, resentment, and inter-Korean sentiment that contributed to the demonstrations, we might have written more authoritatively about their end.

Simply put, we did not connect all the dots. In terms of comprehensive analysis, we came up short. In truth, this is an endless failing. This chapter's very dissection of the shortcomings of the U.S. media coverage during the 2002–2003 spike in anti-Americanism is guilty of the very same offense. That is, the full story spans a much longer period than I have reviewed. For this essay, I used 2000 as my starting point. But one easily could have gone back further, putting an even broader sweep of history on the doorstep of current events.

This is a real occupational hazard when reporting on events in South Korea—in fact, in any Asian country: the deep historical roots of Asian relations inevitably complicate the emotions of the day. For example, South Korean nationalism is periodically fueled by news in Japan: the discovery that Japanese textbooks present a whitewashed account of World War II, a racist remark by a Japanese politician, or yet another visit by the Japanese prime minister to a Yasukuni Shrine for the war dead. These events, while significant in South Korea, are puzzlingly trivial to most Western readers. And even when they do make the Western news, rarely is enough historical background included to make them comprehensible, as most editors assume any story that requires five or six paragraphs of history will lose readers. As a result, history is relegated to tomes that appeal to a small number of experts with unquenchable enthusiasm for the topic.

Most coverage of foreign affairs for a domestic mass market is likely to be parochial to some extent, and U.S. newspaper reporters' coverage of the Koreas was (and is) no exception. We often wrote stories about events on the peninsula from the perspective of how those events would affect American interests,

American policy, American troops, or the American role in the region. The North Korean missile threat became a big story when it included long-range missiles that were seemingly capable of reaching U.S. territory. The South Korean election took on more importance in U.S. news pages when the leading candidate sharply criticized the United States. Korean nationalism became a story when it was manifest in anti-American demonstrations. It would be snooty to find fault with this tendency. It is very much human nature to be most interested in events that affect us personally, and newspapers are called the popular press because they reflect the interests of their readers.

Having already pleaded guilty to the charge of parochialism, let me offer at least a mild defense: U.S. newspapers are less parochial than those of many other nations. American reporters in the region wrote stories not only on events that affected the United States but also on facets of the Koreas and Korean society that were interesting in their own right. And some credit should be given to any newspaper that goes to the expense of maintaining staff writers in foreign countries. At thirty-five cents a newspaper, I doubt my stories from Asia ever sold enough copies to pay the rent in the bureaus from which I filed them.

The first "sale" a reporter must make is to his editor. There is inevitably a tension between reporters, who must become enthused and immersed in their subject, and editors, who must judge a story's worth with a more sober eye. I have never met a newspaper reporter who did not think a great majority of his or her stories belonged on the front page, and who was not frustrated when the editors did not always agree.

Having said that, editors at the major newspapers are neither shallow nor uninterested in good stories. Quite the contrary: most have extensive knowledge of the regions they oversee, and many are experienced former correspondents themselves. I never proposed a Korean story to my editors that did not receive a considered hearing, a thoughtful response, and—nine times out of ten—a go-ahead to do the reporting and write. Sometimes the idea did not survive objective reporting, and sometimes editors suggested that a story be shortened, refocused, rewritten, or even expanded before it got into the paper. But the old cliché of a bored editor simply rejecting a story for lack of curiosity or understanding is not true in the foreign departments of my paper, the *Washington Post*, or the others included in this book.

In fact, there was a large appetite for Korea stories at my paper, and my editors were always eager for more. Though I was based in Tokyo—the *Washington Post* correspondent's beat straddles both Japan and the Koreas—my editors always encouraged me to spend time in South Korea. When I was not in the country, our gifted and indefatigable South Korean special correspondent, Joohee Cho, did the writing and reporting. When I was there, she guided me—one of a parade of *Washington Post* correspondents—through the vagaries of Korean society and politics.

But even with the superb work of Cho and other colleagues, reporting on the Koreas was and is inevitably affected by matters that have little to do with pure news judgments. Reporters go on vacation. They are busy with other stories. They may sidestep an assignment if they get sick, or for family reasons, when they should be on the beat. Their editors may suddenly send them off to other regions, or confine them to their desks because of an end-of-year cutback in the travel budget. The wire services are an invaluable backstop, but wire stories usually get less attention and space than staff-written pieces. In the end, the old cliché is true: like hot dogs, journalism should not be watched too closely in the making. It is a messy process influenced by chance as much as anything. A strictly mathematical analysis of word count and numbers of stories will not necessarily account for this. There is no question that U.S. news interest in the Koreas has waxed and waned through the years, just as it does in nearly every region. Sometimes the Korea story justified more coverage than it received, and sometimes it received more coverage than it justified. The first drafts of history, as Gi-Wook Shin suggests, are often very rough.

THE EXPERIENCES OF A BUSINESS JOURNALIST IN SOUTH KOREA

Martin Fackler

My experience covering business in South Korea began, appropriately enough, with Samsung. As a journalist working mostly in Japan and China since the 1990s, I had noticed South Korea's economic rise but had never had a chance to write about the country. So when I joined the *New York Times* in 2005 as the Tokyo-based business correspondent, a job that includes South Korea in its bailiwick, my first urge was to write about how South Korean companies had broken into autos and electronics—global industries long dominated by Japan. My first call was to Samsung Electronics, the most visible Korean company.

Samsung's response surprised me. Japanese companies tended to be coldly uninterested or even flustered when I approached them. Samsung, by contrast, immediately engaged me. Not long after the call, I was seated at a tony French restaurant in Tokyo with the then newly hired head of Samsung public relations (a former diplomat and Blue House adviser). Soon I was on my first reporting trip to South Korea, my schedule packed with interviews of a half-dozen Samsung executives and tours of Samsung factories and design studios. Other companies proved similarly receptive.

Thus began my contact with the schizophrenic world of corporate South Korea. Companies that seemed open and welcoming at first would at times show a very different face. I would experience my share of frustrations and snubs, particularly when reporting on politically sensitive issues such as family succession and corruption among South Korea's *chaebol* business conglomerates. For instance, I received a very different reception at Samsung when I wrote a story about an investigation into whether Samsung Group's chairman, Lee Kun-hee, had used a complex stock scheme to transfer its control to his children (he would later resign).

This mix of disarming openness and prickly defensiveness has been the defining feature of my experiences writing about business and corporate issues in South Korea. And this split personality seems to point to broader tensions within the country, between the pluralistic potential of one of East Asia's most genuinely democratic political systems and a stubborn clannishness characterized by the secretive and shadowy powers of the *chaebol*.

Whenever I am asked to identify the factors that have defined my coverage of South Korea, this apparent contradiction has been a constant, underlying theme. The other themes discussed in this book—anti-Americanism and nationalism—have likewise made their presence felt. But my coverage has also been shaped by other factors on my side, that is, the side of the media.

Some of these are obvious and long-standing, like the fact that South Korea must live in the shadows of two far larger news stories, Japan and China. Other factors are due to recent structural changes in the newspaper industry itself, brought about by the disruptive and transformative arrival of the Internet. Then there are the challenges that will always be part and parcel of the work of the foreign correspondent: how to present a distant land and unfamiliar people in a way that is intelligible and engaging to people back home—in my case, to readers who might be standing on a crowded Manhattan subway or sipping coffee on the Upper West Side.

In my experience, the key has been to maintain a strong focus on issues that are of clear interest to Americans. This has pushed my coverage toward industries and companies that have built large presences in American consumer markets, such as Samsung, LG Electronics, and Hyundai Motors. It also leads to topics of innate interest to American readers, such as cutting-edge South Korean technology or the experiences of American businessmen and investors in South Korea.

Still, on the ground, it is the vibrant but not completely democratic nature of South Korea that constantly confronts me. And this is how broader themes such as democracy impact something as apparently distant from the realm of politics as business reporting. While South Korean civil society remains a work in progress, it is unquestionably one of the most robust in all of Northeast Asia, rivaled perhaps only by Taiwan. South Korea appears to have a far livelier political discourse than, say, Japan, where democracy is decades older, and certainly than Communist China. (In China, I was a general news reporter, without a focus on economics.) In the press, the big South Korean newspapers still pull their punches, but the arrival of alternatives such as the "participatory citizen journalism" of the online OhmyNews has spiced up media behavior in ways unseen in the establishment-dominated Japanese media.

As a result, South Korean companies appear more accustomed to dealing with a contentious press, at least when compared with their Japanese and Chinese counterparts. For the average Japanese company, "media" begin and end with the *Nihon Keizai Shimbun*, Japan's largest business daily. By contrast, large Korean companies seem more aware of the importance of global media, particularly big U.S. and British publications. This might reflect these companies' greater dependence on export markets, given the relatively small size of South Korea's home market. And, as relative newcomers to the global market, they may be more proactive in establishing a positive image for their brands among overseas consumers.

In my coverage, this relative openness has led me to present big South Korean companies as slightly savvier and more international than many of their Japanese counterparts, whether or not that is actually the case. In my stories about the cell-phone industry, for instance, I tend to portray the South Korean manufacturers Samsung, LG Electronics, and even the smaller Pantech Group as nimbler in catching new American and European trends. In part, this reflects the simple reality that South Korean cell-phone companies have a big chunk of the world market, while the Japanese, despite their early technological lead, do not. But I must admit it also made a difference when, for example, Pantech gave me a highly detailed tour of its cell-phone plant in Gimpo. The most welcoming and media-friendly Japanese companies have never let me within throwing distance of a cell-phone factory.

This simple issue of access makes a big difference in coverage. Japan's most open technology companies, such as Sharp or Toshiba, have allowed me to view their flat-panel or semiconductor production lines only from behind panels of glass; I have never been permitted near the most sensitive parts of the manufacturing process. By contrast, LG once let me spend an afternoon watching every step of production at a plasma TV factory in Gumi. Just being able to include a physical description of the LG factory makes it much more likely that LG will be featured more prominently in a story than a Japanese company.

In addition to themes of business savvy and transparency, topics related to South Korean nationalism and anti-Americanism appear in my coverage, though the latter far less frequently. The issue tends to show up in stories about the American economic presence in South Korea, such as the free trade agreement signed in 2007 between Seoul and Washington (the KORUS FTA) or the social backlash against American investment funds such as Lone Star, which arrived in the wake of the 1997 financial crisis to take over ailing South Korean banks and other companies.

As a theme, anti-Americanism is unavoidable because it permeates the rhetoric of South Korean opponents of the KORUS FTA or foreign hedge funds. For example, in covering the opponents of Lone Star and other American funds, I visited offices of activists and social groups festooned with posters that showed torn American flags and large fists on the head of President George W. Bush. In their writings and speeches, these activists describe Lone Star as a symbol of American economic domination, and a form of cultural imperialism through which the United States tries to impose its brand of capitalism upon smaller South Korea. Resistance to Lone Star, according to those who oppose it, represents nothing less than a heroic defense of South Korean identity and autonomy.

Move beyond the rhetoric, however, and new questions arise. The biggest is trying to determine exactly how anti-American the anti-Americans really are. These same groups that demonize Lone Star and cowboy capitalism will also sit down for hours to carefully and amiably answer the questions of an American journalist. Without prompting, they eagerly emphasize their affiliations with American antiglobalization groups, which actually supplied many of the anti-Bush caricatures. In fact, members of these groups freely admitted to me that many of their anti-American arguments originate in the American antiglobalization movement.

Given these contrasts, I often find myself reluctant to characterize such activities as simply anti-American. I felt the same ambivalence when looking into

71

last year's explosively popular South Korean monster movie *Gwoemul* (*The Host*), about a mutated creature that devours people along the Han River. For a time, it seemed everyone was eager to tell me that the monster was a metaphor for the United States and its carnivorous lack of concern for the interests of the Korean people, from the North as well as the South. But I concluded that this comparison was not meant to provoke or even reject the United States. Rather, it reflected a desire to assert an identity that was independent and free of the United States, which has had a strong, almost paternalistic presence in South Korea.

On the other hand, nationalism is a recurrent and common theme in my coverage. It appears even in ostensibly corporate stories such as those on Samsung or new South Korean technologies. One of my first big stories out of South Korea examined the role of the Ministry of Information and Communication in the nation's cell-phone industry and its pushes to make South Korea the top producer of new technologies such as CDMA (the base technology of all so-called third-generation cell-phone networks) and, more recently, wireless Internet and high-speed fourth-generation communication networks. The story was intended to explain South Korea's rise as a leader in global cell phones. But the very nature of a government-led push into new technologies and industries made economic nationalism the obvious choice for the story's broader thematic framework.

A less cut-and-dried example was a profile I wrote of Samsung in April 2006. Most corporate profiles tend to focus on microeconomic issues, including influential managers, business rivals, and the company's place in the broader industry. But with Samsung, I found a company that occupies such an enormous position in South Korea's economy, and the nation's popular consciousness, that I ended up casting it as a sort of national champion. The same was true of one of Samsung's key future challenges that I identified in the story: whether or not it can make the jump into the pantheon of global technology brands, joining the likes of Apple and Sony, by creating an iconic breakthrough product like the iPod or the Walkman. This struck me as an important issue not just for Samsung but also for South Korea more broadly. I presented Samsung's quest as part of a national desire to advance from imitator to high-tech innovator.

Here I perhaps need to make another confession: a big reason why I write about economic nationalism is personal interest. I came of age during Japan's 1980s economic rise. In college, I avidly read stories by David E. Sanger (who contributed chapter 11 of this book) and James Sterngold, as well as books by Chalmers Johnson and Daniel I. Okimoto[1] that describe Japan's state-guided brand of capitalism and how it differs from its American analogue. Ever since, economic nationalism has been my overarching interest, both personally and professionally. In my coverage of South Korea, my enthusiasm for the subject has led me to delve into the state's role in development and into what extent South Korea has followed the Japan model.

I also enjoy comparing South Korea and Japan's very different reactions to their separate economic crises in the 1990s. Japan adopted a gradualist approach to fixing its banking system, which limited social dislocation but arguably cost the nation a decade of growth. South Korea undertook an American-prescribed swift and painful cleanup of the banking system, which put society through the wringer but also apparently fixed problems more quickly.

The personal interests and quirks of a writer can play a big role in determining the choice of topics and tone of coverage, and must be a frustratingly elusive variable in academic studies of press coverage. But alas, this is not a perfect world, and enticing as the thought may be, personal interest does not exclusively determine what we write. I would characterize my coverage as the product of a convergence of personal interests and observations, combined with a host of external factors, some of which I mentioned earlier.

The influence of some of these factors might not be immediately apparent, but it can in fact be profound. First and foremost has been the rise of the Internet, which has clobbered newspaper readership and thus advertising revenues. The most obvious impact of this revenue decrease has been the shutting of overseas bureaus, which has not altered coverage of South Korea so much as reduced it. Overseas bureaus are easy targets for corporate bean counters because they tend to be very expensive. This pullout has hit Seoul and Tokyo (from which both the *New York Times* and the *Washington Post* cover South Korea) particularly hard because both cities have high living costs. In the short time that I have been involved in South Korea, I have seen the *Los Angeles Times* close its Seoul bureau and watched *Time* magazine shrink its presence. Even the handful of newspapers, including the *New York Times*, that have maintained their overall number of overseas bureaus have been forced to shift resources out of Northeast Asia to offset the enormous costs of covering the war in Iraq.

The newspaper industry's financial difficulties have also affected news coverage in other ways. One change that has had huge impact is the shrinking "news hole," the amount of space in the newspaper available for stories. Newspapers including both the *New York Times* and my previous employer, the *Wall Street Journal*, have cut costs by reducing their number of pages and in some cases their page size. This has put space in the newspaper at a premium. As a result, fewer stories appear in print, affecting both the amount of coverage and the choices of topics and themes to cover. For editors, the diminishing space makes them more selective in choosing which stories to use. Reporters, for their part, must conceive stories with an even closer eye on slipping past the gatekeepers and into the ever-shrinking news hole.

On an average day, the business section of the *New York Times* might carry three or four overseas stories. This stands in contrast to just five years ago, when the paper devoted an entire separate section to international business. In the current business section, a daily news story out of South Korea must compete for these few coveted slots with events elsewhere in the world, including areas of higher interest to Americans (such as China and India), or in more familiar locales (such as London or Paris). To run a longer enterprise piece about South Korea on the first business page—the most choice and visible real estate in the business section—the article must also compete with big domestic stories, whether Google, George Soros, or General Motors, all of which are far closer to home for editors and readers.

Clearing these sorts of hurdles means satisfying editors that American readers will find a story sufficiently compelling. Unlike China or India, South Korea is not large enough to command readers' interest just by its name alone. And no matter how fast South Korea grows, it will never become large enough to reshape the global economy, or place the entire planet at environmental risk, as China stands to do.

As a reporter, I must find different strategies for getting South Korean business stories into the newspaper, a task that is not unique to South Korean coverage. Making a tale from an alien land resonate with readers back home lies at the core of the foreign correspondent's craft. At the *Wall Street Journal*, we used to do this by asking ourselves whether a story would appeal to a used-car salesman in Des Moines or a Kinko's copy shop clerk—in other words, to average Americans with no background or intrinsic interest in our corner of Asia. This criterion pushed us to write stories that were somehow relevant to our readers' lives, or just compelling enough on an emotional or intellectual level to convince the proverbial Kinko's man that he should take five minutes out of his day to read them.

In my coverage of South Korea, one easy strategy has been name recognition: writing about Korean brands and products that Americans recognize and possibly even own. Obviously, this has pushed my coverage toward the big electronics companies and automakers, particularly Samsung and Hyundai Motors. This same strategy has led me to give relative emphasis to more consumer-focused products, such as cell phones, flat-panel televisions, and computer memory chips, in which South Korean companies are big global players. Conversely, and despite their arguable importance, I have given less attention to other domestic Korean industries, such as banking.

Could big American newspapers include more business coverage of South Korea in their pages? Yes, but not until Americans start buying newspapers again, or publishers like the *New York Times* migrate entirely to the Internet, with its limitless news hole. Are there shortcomings in the current coverage? Of course. How would I rate the overall U.S. media coverage of South Korea? Mediocre, but at least we are still in the game. Even with the bureau closures, the American media presence in South Korea is large, matched only, perhaps, by the Japanese, who are geographically much closer. I believe that this continued presence—borne out by robust demand for South Korea coverage at my publication and others—reflects South Korea's still relatively large place in the American popular consciousness and, in turn, continued interest in its national story for the foreseeable future.

Note

[1] See Chalmers A. Johnson, *MITI and the Japanese Miracle: The Growth of Industrial Policy, 1925–1975* (Stanford, CA: Stanford University Press, 1982), and Daniel I. Okimoto, *Between MITI and the Market: Japanese Industrial Policy for High Technology* (Stanford, CA: Stanford University Press, 1989).

REPORTING ON NORTH KOREA AND THE NUCLEAR PROBLEM

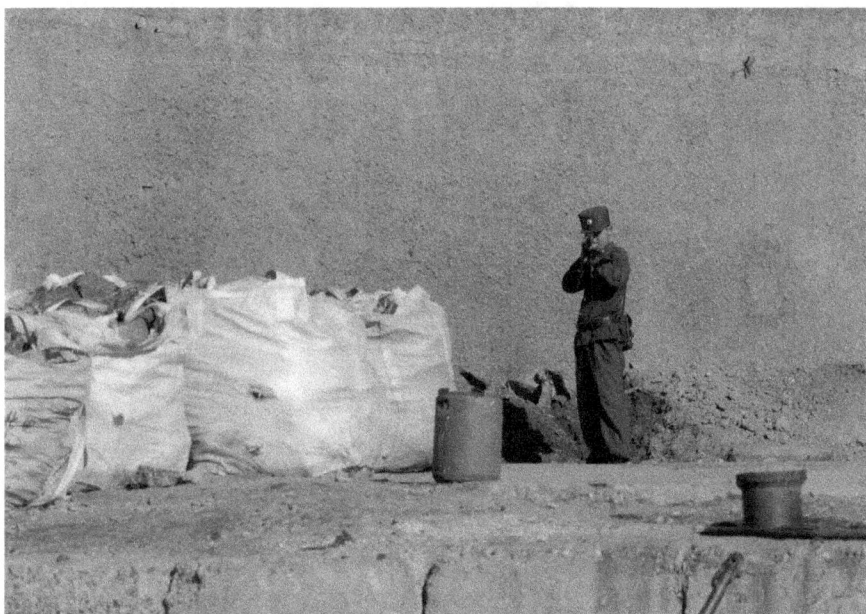

A North Korean soldier points a gun at a photographer on the banks of the Yalu River near the North Korean town of Sinuiju, opposite the Chinese border city of Dandong. *Credit:* Reuters/Stringer Shanghai.

THE CHALLENGES OF
COVERING NORTH KOREA

Donald A. L. Macintyre

On my last visit to Pyongyang, in 2005, I bumped into a North Korean government official I knew. I had spent some time with him three years earlier when I joined a group of Japanese on a trip to North Korea. An amiable, well-groomed man probably in his mid-forties, he was in charge of escorting the Japanese visitors around the country. Since that trip, I had seen him on CNN, translating for the "dear leader," Kim Jong-il, when Japanese prime minister Junichiro Koizumi visited Pyongyang in 2002. Now here he was, coming out of a hotel restaurant just as I was heading in.

He greeted me with an enthusiastic handshake, although I was pretty sure he was not a big fan of foreigner reporters. As we chatted in front of the restaurant, I asked him what he thought of the article I had written about my 2002 trip. To my surprise, he told me that not all of it was unsatisfactory. Sensing a rare chance to cement an unusual contact, I casually suggested we get together for a cup of coffee the next day. My North Korean official was not going to reveal any nuclear secrets (nor was he likely to have any), but I hoped to glean a few insights into the workings of his opaque country. After mumbling some vague excuses, however, he turned me down. We shook hands and I have not seen him since.

So much for my potential source of news from the axis of evil. In North Korea, an unscripted meeting with a foreign journalist can have extremely serious consequences for a government official. The country remains maddeningly paranoid when it comes to foreigners—the foreign press in particular. During my 2005 trip to North Korea, my minder—I will call him Mr. Choi—made it clear that he didn't trust me. The foreign journalist assures you he plans to write a positive story, Choi told me with an angry scowl, but when he gets back home, he writes sensational stories that make North Korea look bad.

Mr. Choi's attitude was typical of North Korean officialdom, and throughout the trip he did his best to show us as little of his country as he could. Pyongyang lets in very few journalists, and this presents an enormous and much-discussed obstacle to North Korea reporting. Foreign journalists' lack of access to the country leads, in turn, to a bigger problem: lack of access to North Koreans. Without in-country informants, journalists have to source most stories to U.S. government officials and to North Korean defectors living outside the country. Much of Washington's information about North Korea comes from satellite and others forms of electronic surveillance. And stories sourced to the U.S. officials who read these electronic tea leaves tend to focus on policy. But to write about North Korea as a country, rather than a policy issue, journalists must rely on defector testimony. In this chapter, I will consider some of the difficulties presented by defector sources and why the recent decline of foreign news coverage in the United States will likely damage North Korea coverage in particular.

I know of no Western journalists who have sources in North Korea in the usual sense of the word. Meeting a North Korean official may help you get into the country, but not much more. In stories about North Korea, "sources" are never North Korean government officials. On rare occasions, a correspondent may secure an interview with a government official, usually from the foreign ministry. But every official encounter in North Korea takes place under the watchful gaze of government minders, at least some of whom are intelligence agents. Journalists cannot even get economic statistics for government bureaucracies—they stopped publishing them years ago.

Evil Americans are a staple of Pyongyang propaganda, so the average North Korean may simply be afraid of American-looking Westerners. As envoys of a U.S. ally and the reviled former colonial power in the peninsula, Japanese reporters are also regarded with suspicion. North Koreans are certainly afraid of the consequences of talking to foreigners, particularly journalists, without permission. You will not find a North Korean who wants to get you alone to talk. Nor will you find an intellectual who will invite you into his home to tell you, over a cup of tea, about what is really happening in the country, as you might in, say, Myanmar. This reticence is a measure of just how hard the regime has worked to isolate its citizens. A North Korean friend of mine, now based in Seoul, once told me about the preparations for the 1989 World Youth Festival in Pyongyang. The regime wanted to compete with South Korea after Seoul had successfully hosted the 1988 Olympics, but it was concerned about the influx of foreign visitors poking around the capital and asking nosy questions. The regime's solution: issue a booklet to residents of Pyongyang instructing them on what to say to foreigners and how to deflect political questions. It included a few tips on praising the regime.

Getting into the country does not allow you, the journalist, to burst the bubble. You may break away from your minders long enough to talk, for example, to a vendor at a street kiosk. You will be lucky, however, if she even makes a few bland comments about the product she is selling. This reticence so pervades the country that many stories datelined Pyongyang read like travelogues full of anecdotes about the weirdness of the place but with little insight into what people's lives are really like. Journalists often share the perspective of the tourist who happened to sit at my breakfast table one morning in Pyongyang. His hobby was traveling to the remotest and strangest corners of the earth. "North Korea," he observed, "is like the moon, with people."

By and large, North Korean people will not talk to outsiders. It was only in the 1990s that some of the denizens of Planet North Korea started to flee their home and tell their stories to the wider world. Until then, few North Koreans had abandoned their country, which is one reason why so little was written about what was going on inside it. Increasingly, the famine that began in the early 1990s drove North Koreans across the Tumen River, to search for food and jobs in the Korean-speaking area of China. Most eventually returned home or remained in China. But a growing number embarked on the difficult and dangerous journey across China to Southeast Asia, where they sought help at South Korean embassies. From fewer than 1,000 in the mid-1990s, the number of North Koreans in the South reached more than 12,000 by 2007 and continues to rise steadily.

This number is still pathetically small when compared with the thousands of refugees that the United States and European countries take in every year. Nevertheless, as a result of this steady influx, a significant population of North Koreans now lives outside North Korea, in places where they can tell their stories more or less freely (although some are reluctant to speak because they have left family members behind). Many have told their tales to foreign journalists; some have even testified before the U.S. Congress. They have increased our store of knowledge about North Korea immensely and created opportunities to cover North Korea as a country, rather than as simply a policy issue.

For journalists, however, the use of refugee and defector testimony poses problems. In his award-winning exposé of how the Bush administration used propaganda to sell the Iraq war (published in *Rolling Stone* magazine), James Bamford describes a CIA encounter with an Iraqi defector before the war.[1] The defector, Adnan Ihsan Saeed al-Haideri, claimed to be an engineer who had helped stash tons of biological, chemical, and nuclear weapons around Iraq. Some of it was hidden in Baghdad, under the country's biggest medical facility, he told CIA agents. It was exactly the kind of smoking gun the administration needed to make the case for war. According to Bamford, correspondent Judith Miller ran a story based on this testimony on the front page of the *New York Times*.

What Miller's sources apparently didn't tell her was that al-Haideri had failed a lie detector test administered by CIA agents at a Thai beach resort. Or that his handler, Ahmad Chalabi, had spent a decade trying to drag the United States into a war against Saddam Hussein. Like much of the prewar defector testimony on Iraq, al-Haideri's story was a fabrication.

I had followed the prewar intelligence story and its aftermath, but Bamford's story caught my attention—and gave me a jolt. I too had interviewed a defector at a Thai beach resort: a North Korean, not an Iraqi. I did not give him a lie detector test, of course. The whole scenario made me wonder if we were exercising due diligence on stories that rely on North Korean defectors.

The North Korean whom I interviewed told an extraordinary story. He had walked around his northeastern hometown of Hoeryong with a concealed video recorder, secretly taping a marketplace, buildings, and a factory. He also filmed protest banners, one pinned on a wall and another strung under a bridge, which called for the overthrow of the Kim government. "Down with Kim Jong-il!" screamed hand-painted letters in red ink. "People, let's all rise up and drive out the dictatorship!" The final scene of the video showed antigovernment graffiti scrawled over an official poster of Kim dressed in a general's uniform.

A South Korean nongovernmental organization (NGO) played the video at a press conference in Seoul. It was dramatic stuff, seemingly the first-ever footage of antigovernment activity inside North Korea. North Korea has no known dissident movement—it is still too dangerous to speak out. Nobody has stepped forward in the way that writers and other intellectuals did in Eastern Europe and the Soviet Union. The near-total absence of public protest in North Korea made this man's story potentially very significant.

Defectors from Hoeryong confirmed that the footage was shot in their hometown. Jerky and erratic, it looked as if it had been filmed secretly under difficult conditions. Yet the video raised difficult questions. The head of the South Korean NGO that obtained the video said a Japanese television station had paid the NGO to run the footage, which made it seem more of a fundraising exercise—and created an obvious conflict of interest for the NGO. I was also troubled to learn that the North Korean who had shot the footage had pinned up the protest banners himself. If this was dissent, it was dissent staged for an audience. More alarm bells went off when I heard that the NGO had ties to a conservative lawmaker in Washington. After the press conference, I asked the head of the NGO if I could meet the North Korean who had shot the video. He said he might be able to arrange it.

A few months later, I caught up with Mr. Lee, as I will call him, in Thailand. Lee told me that he had fled North Korea after the authorities launched a crackdown to find the author of the video. Over the course of two days, he gave me a detailed account of his life and the events that led him to carry out what in North Korea would be considered an act of treason, punishable by death. After his military service, Lee had returned home during the 1990s famine to find his father dead and his mother starving. He went into business in the nascent black market—as did thousands of other North Koreans—when food rations from the state stopped coming. Lee fell in with some black market video traders who were unhappy with the situation in North Korea, particularly the growing corruption. The group claimed to have connections in Pyongyang and other cities. Eventually they provided him with a video recorder. He told me how he and his friends had planned the operation around a kitchen table, then gone out one day and shot the video. On a satellite map of Hoeryong, he showed me the route he had taken. He wanted to show the world what was going on in North Korea, he said, and enlist the international community's help in getting rid of Kim Jong-il. Details of the story jibed with many accounts of life in North Korea that I had heard from other defectors. If it was a deception, it was a very elaborate one. But how I wish I could have hooked him up to a lie detector.

I could not escape the feeling that selling videos to foreigners might be just another of Lee's businesses ventures. Japanese television was willing to pay large sums for footage of North Korea, the more sensational the better. He said he had received a few thousand dollars for his efforts. A reliable source told me the NGO received quite a bit more. Lee's prodemocracy activist stance might have been sincere, or it might have been shtick. Either way, it raised the value of his video. Was he really part of a network of like-minded activists? He seemed convinced he was, but he had no way to prove it.

At the time, I was unable to answer all of these questions adequately, so I wrote only a short piece for *Time* magazine, citing the NGO as the source of the footage. My editors did not think it was worth flying me to Thailand to pursue the story. *Time* was examining its costs more closely, and the questions I have mentioned made the investment a risky proposition. I decided to go to Thailand and probe Lee's story anyway, at my own expense. Had I not been working on a book project at the time, I doubt I would have paid my own way to Thailand to sit in a hotel for two days talking to a defector, while a glorious tropical sun beat down outside. But if Lee really was part of an emerging dissident movement, I believed the story was fascinating and important.

North Korea is supposed to be an oppressive totalitarian state where dissent is impossible. If Lee was merely an entrepreneur who had sniffed out a market for videos documenting opposition to the regime in North Korea, his story was still compelling. Communist North Korea is not supposed to be producing entrepreneurs. Doing illegal business for self-profit may not be an act of dissent, but it certainly represents a repudiation of the state's ideological foundations. Lee's actions, whatever their motives, said something important about what was going on in North Korea.

I do not blame my editors for dropping the story. They were willing to pursue leads on North Korea up to a point. But a profile of this subject might not have panned out. We did not know if he was for real—in fact, I am still not sure. What we did know was that there was a limited appetite for such stories in New York, where the domestic edition of *Time* is edited. With the exception of stories about Kim Jong-il's taste in women and wine, North Korea was (and is) a hard sell. Unless events are likely to have a direct impact on the United States, there is often little interest. When North Korea launched a missile that could possibly hit Alaska, the magazine covered it. But *Time*'s Washington bureau always seemed distracted by the Washington agenda, particularly what was happening in Iraq. And even in Asia, there were limits to the resources we could devote to vetting stories built on defector testimony.

Another vexing case based on defector testimony centered on allegations that North Korea was carrying out chemical tests on prisoners. I first heard the story in 2004 from a respected human rights activist in Seoul. He handed me a sheaf of papers that proved, he said, that prisoners had been transferred from a North Korean prison to a chemical plant, where they would be used for testing chemical weapons. The papers bore the official seal of the North Korean state security agency. Mr. Park, as he calls himself, told me an electrical engineer who worked at the chemical plant had stolen them and smuggled them out of North Korea.

Were these documents real? At *Time*, we immediately tried to vet them. I showed them to several defectors who had been in the military and high positions in the bureaucracy, and they immediately noticed problems. Some of the terminology looked South Korean. The official seals and the signature were not in the right place. The name on the state security seal was out of date: the agency had adopted a new name several years earlier.

I took the materials to defector Ahn Myong-chul, who had once worked as a guard at Camp 22 (a notorious North Korean prison for political prisoners), where the documents had allegedly been signed. Ahn had never witnessed experiments on humans at the camp. But he said everybody knew something horrible was going on. Russian trucks with no license plates would leave loaded with prisoners and come back empty, soiled with excrement and vomit. Ahn recognized the signature at the bottom of the document. The man had held a lower-level position but could have risen to become head of security after Ahn defected. Ahn's first reaction: the document was "70 percent" convincing. "Where did you get it?" he asked with amazement.

Finally, I took the papers to an acquaintance who had analyzed many North Korean documents. I explained the problems defectors had identified. After taking a careful look, he declared that the documents were probably genuine. The discrepancies were likely a function of Camp 22's distance from Pyongyang—officials out in the provinces were not following the bureaucratic procedures laid down in the capital. Perhaps they had lost the new official seal after the state security agency's name changed and just pulled the old one out of the drawer. There was no way to be sure unless you could get more documents from the same place. The bottom line was that one could not confirm the papers were real, but neither could one say that they were fakes.

Time decided, with regret, not to run the story. The BBC, which had obtained the same documents, did run it. I am not convinced that the BBC had definitive confirmation. The story may still turn out to be accurate, but if the documents are declared fakes, the effort to shed light on human rights issues in North Korea will suffer. Defector testimony will become an even tougher sell.

Such a development would be unfortunate. In my view, defector testimony, used judiciously, can be extremely valuable. At *Time*, I wrote several stories about how traders and entrepreneurs are transforming the North Korean economy at the grassroots level. Rather than asking North Koreans about Kim Jong-il's grooming habits or where he stashed his nukes, I would question them about daily life. How much did it cost you to buy rice in the local market? How do you make a living? What are conditions like at the local school? In this kind of story, defector testimony is much safer—no one has any incentive to exaggerate, except perhaps about how tough things are inside the country. By talking to enough people, you can winnow out the inaccuracies, just as you do in any reporting.

Trying to verify North Korean documents and defector testimony takes time and money. At least three-quarters of the stories we heard from defectors ended up on the proverbial cutting-room floor. I would like to think we did a service to readers by printing the few stories we could confirm and killing the stories we could not. What worries me is that carefully reported stories about what is going on inside North Korea will become even rarer as U.S. media organizations cut budgets for overseas news. And North Korea is not as expensive to cover as Iraq, which requires a significant commitment of time and money. How many inaccurate stories will run because news organizations lack both the time to vet them and the experienced correspondents on the ground to conduct the vetting? How many stories will simply never be written?

Time magazine and the *Los Angeles Times* have both recently closed their bureaus in Seoul (the *Los Angeles Times* has since combined its Tokyo and Seoul bureaus, and now covers both Japan and South Korea from Seoul). Only three Western newspapers, the *Financial Times*, the *Wall Street Journal*, and the *International Herald Tribune*, still maintain full-time correspondents dedicated to covering the Korean Peninsula. Meanwhile, publications such as the *Washington Post* have fewer Tokyo-based reporters on staff who can fly to Seoul to cover events. The result? The United States will become more dependent on South Korean sources for news about North Korea. Some of that reporting may be good, but it is often politicized.

This chain of events is part of a much broader problem in journalism. The business model for journalism is broken, and no one has figured out how to fix it. The consequences go far beyond diminishing journalists' job security. In his recent book *Bad News*, veteran CBS correspondent Tom Fenton laments the decline of foreign news coverage in the United States and the danger it represents to U.S. national security. Fenton argues that the media failed to alert the country to the impending catastrophe of September 11. In the two decades before the attack on the World Trade Towers, newspapers and broadcast networks slashed foreign coverage by 70 to 80 percent, he estimates. The reasons are complex but boil down to this: foreign news is expensive, and network executives do not believe the American public has an appetite for it. Fenton says he and others had been tracking al-Qaeda stories for a decade, but few of them made it onto the evening news because bosses in New York did not consider them newsworthy.[2]

Bad News opens with a chilling description of a visit that Mohammed Atta, a key figure in the 9/11 attacks, paid to a U.S. Department of Agriculture loan office. After the loan officer turned down Atta's request for money to finance the purchase of a twin-engine, six-passenger aircraft that he planned to fit with a giant chemical tank, Atta tried to buy an aerial photo of Washington that was hanging on the wall of the official's office. He asked her to point out the White House and the Pentagon. He even lectured her about al-Qaeda and its leader, Osama bin Laden. She did not report the incident to the FBI until after 9/11, she said, because she had not heard of bin Laden. According to Fenton, al-Qaeda was not mentioned once by the three evening news broadcasts in the three months leading up to 9/11.[3]

What happens when a defector comes out of North Korea claiming that Kim Jong-il is dead? Or asserts that the regime has transferred plutonium to Iran? Will the Western media be up to the task of figuring out what such events mean, if anything? What about the coverage of other, more subtle changes in North Korea, such as the development of a fledgling market economy? The international community is at a critical point in its efforts to deal with Pyongyang. Stories out of Washington that address North Korea as a policy issue and a national security problem will continue to flow. But stories out of North Korea told by North Koreans might not. That would probably suit Pyongyang just fine. The rest of us should be worried that shutting off the information tap, even if it is producing only a trickle, could contribute to miscalculations in a corner of the world where the stakes couldn't be higher.

Notes

[1] James Bamford, "The Man Who Sold the War," *Rolling Stone*, November 17, 2005, http://www.rollingstone.com/politics/story/8798997/the_man_who_sold_the_war.

[2] Tom Fenton, *Bad News: The Decline of Reporting, the Business of News, and the Danger to Us All* (New York: Collins Living, 2005), 2.

[3] Fenton, *Bad News*, 4.

TALES OF THE HERMIT KINGDOM

Anna Fifield

As we stood in the sunshine on the northern side of the Joint Security Area at Panmunjom in April 2007, Lt. Col. Ri Kwang-chol summed up his country's attitude toward us and our profession. His smiles started to wear thin as we peppered him with questions on the way into the demilitarized zone (DMZ), and after one too many difficult inquiries, he finally spoke in plain language. "I know that it is your responsibility to ask these questions," he said in a steely monotone, "but it is my personal opinion that journalists from Western countries are not reliable." That was the end of that.

Indeed, North Korean officials and Western journalists have little in common. North Korea uses information as a tool for control—trying to regulate the information that North Koreans receive about the world and the information that the world receives about North Korea. Journalists, on the other hand, support the free, unfettered flow of information, information that we can check and source and reliably convey to our readers. These contradictory impulses make writing about North Korea akin to assembling a monochrome jigsaw puzzle. It takes a long time to put the pieces together, and even when you manage to make the pieces fit, it can be hard to discern the image. But since North Korea's October 2006 nuclear test, it has been increasingly important to try to understand the country and its military goals.

Once just another repressive state with a quirky leader, North Korea now looms large as a security threat. The 2006 test proved not only that the country has the ability to make a crude nuclear device but that it had reprocessed enough plutonium to be able to spare six or so kilograms for such an experiment. Because of North Korea's entry into the nuclear club and the increased urgency of finding a way to deal with Kim Jong-il and his regime, international media coverage of North Korea has risen sharply in recent years. Most international newspapers cover the Six-Party Talks and offer readers long, analytical pieces much more regularly than was the case even a decade ago, during the first nuclear crisis, when North Korea was just another tin-pot dictatorship with nuclear ambitions. At the *Financial Times*, the paper for which I write, editors and readers alike are showing renewed fascination for all things North Korean—the economy, society, human rights, and of course, the sheer wackiness of the place. But interest in North Korea tends to fade quickly—the July 2006 missile tests were in the news for only a few days, soon bumped by the Israeli-Lebanese conflict. Indeed, interest in the tests fizzled almost as quickly as the devices tested.

A U.S. State Department official once told me that George W. Bush's administration spent 85 percent of its time thinking about Iraq and Iran, leaving

15 percent for the rest of the world. North Korea therefore competed with hot spots such as China for a sliver of attention. The policy story alone, with its ramifications for global security, could fill that small allotment. But North Korea is much more than a policy story, and it is incumbent on journalists to convey as much as they can about what the country is actually like. We can serve the public interest by showing snapshots of this place—the administrative environment that produced people like chief North Korean nuclear negotiator Kim Kye-gwan, the poverty and terror in which ordinary people are forced to live, and the human tragedy that persists within the country's heavily patrolled borders.

Getting to North Korea

Media organizations pay foreign correspondents to be their "eyes and ears" in the places where the news is happening. But how do you cover North Korea when just getting that brown-and-white North Korean visa stuck into your passport is a considerable feat? About one in every ten attempts I have made to get into North Korea has worked—I was able to visit Pyongyang five times between 2005 and 2008. It is undoubtedly exciting to be a journalist entering North Korea—the scarcity of those visas makes you feel as though you have achieved something just in getting there. But the novelty wears off soon after arriving at Pyongyang airport, where the authorities impose the first of endless restrictions—no cell phones, no laptops with wireless capability, no speaking Korean—and the propaganda begins to flow.

In the course of your visit, a North Korean will inevitably come up to you and say, "Welcome to Pyongyang, the capital of North Korea, created by our Great Leader Kim Il-sung." His purple-shaded sunglasses will instantly give away his affiliation with state security. Soon after getting on the bus to head into the city, you will realize that your itinerary consists largely of visits to bizarre monuments to the personality cult of Kim Il-sung and Kim Jong-il, with very little that could possibly generate news. I find little to write about at Mangyongdae, the purported birthplace of Kim Il-sung. The Workers' Party Monument and the USS *Pueblo*—a U.S. Navy ship captured in 1968 off the North Korean coast and now anchored on the Daedong River in Pyongyang to provide proof of the United States' hostile intentions toward North Korea—likewise fail to inspire. Nor do recitations of the significance of the number of blocks used to make the Juche Tower strike me as front-page news. The frustration builds when you attempt to have things added to your itinerary and are told that it is simply "impossible."

On my most recent visit, in February 2008, I wondered if the North Korean regime actually wanted me to write clichéd stories about the craziness there. To be sure, there is little that is new to show journalists—if there were, the authorities would seize the opportunity to show it to us. But the constant visits to celebrations of the personality cult essentially force us to write about the oddities of the country. Most visas are granted during festivals, when the city is festooned with lights and banners, women glide around in traditional dress, and families picnic beside the Daedong River. This is the North Korea that Kim Jong-il's regime wants the outside world to see, but it is not representative of the actual country

This strategy does seem to work, at least some of the time. During the second run of the Arirang Games in October 2005—a propaganda extravaganza of mass gymnastics, dance, and circus stunts—I was part of a group of Seoul-based journalists who visited Pyongyang at the same time as a group of American adventure travelers. Among them was a man who introduced himself as the "second most well-traveled person on earth." Pyongyang was the only capital he had not visited. Even this seasoned traveler, a California real estate developer with a slew of stories about his trips to the world's most far-flung places, fell for this North Korean trick. "It doesn't look so bad," he told us on the first day of the trip. After a few days of traveling around the city—and more important, several nights in the bar with a group of foreign correspondents—he saw things a little differently. "I didn't think it was that bad—until I talked to you journalists," he told us as we boarded the Air Koryo plane back to Beijing.

North Korea presents journalists with a conundrum. We can get to Pyongyang only sometimes, and we want to report what we see there when we do. We are also aware that what we see is a Potemkin village, a false construct. Pyongyang is not the North Korea I want to report, but I have repeatedly been refused access to the "real North Korea," which includes cities such as Kim Chaek, Wonsan, Chongjin, and Hoeryong. I deal with this frustrating situation by writing articles that expose Pyongyang as a showcase capital, in which events are staged in order to present the country in the best possible light. As much as I can, I make clear that Pyongyang and its choreographed activities do not represent the country as a whole.

Quoting North Koreans is another problem. Much of what they tell us is wrong—that the United States started the Korean War, that the United States continues to keep nuclear weapons in South Korea, that Pyongyang Station is an internationally famous train station. Admittedly, it was difficult to argue this last point after I managed, with two colleagues, to break out of our hotel undetected at two o'clock one morning. There is not enough electricity for street lights in Pyongyang, and the darkness gave us cover as we walked to the station, adding credibility to the North Korean assertion that foreigners from around the world want to visit the stop.

The more reliable answers that North Koreans give us are no less problematic. Journalists can talk only to government-designated people, who undoubtedly go through hours of preparation before they meet us. This is evident in the answers that they give. In April 2007, I posed the same question, at different times, to three different people—my government-appointed guide, the woman who showed us around the USS *Pueblo*, and the guide at the Juche Tower—and received almost exactly identical answers. Specifically, when I asked about the nuclear agreement of February 13, all three parroted an answer about the need for "simultaneous actions," with Washington returning frozen North Korean bank deposits in exchange for Pyongyang shutting down the Yongbyon reactor. Although they were all regurgitating what they had been told to say, I think it is important that journalists report the North Korean perspective; this viewpoint, after all, strongly influences whether the Six-Party Talks stall or progress. But we need to treat North Korean statements in the same way that we treat reports from the Korean Central News Agency—as an integral part of the propaganda.

I have been amazed by the extent to which these guides are prepared for our questions. On a visit to Mount Kumgang shortly after Hurricane Katrina struck the southern United States, I remarked to the North Korean trail guide how devastating the hurricane was. I did this because I know that the North Korean news focuses heavily on natural disasters, in part as a way for the regime to neatly shift blame for problems such as food shortages onto unavoidable natural catastrophes. Even so, I was astounded by the guide's answer. He ranted about how the devastation that Katrina caused underlined the hypocrisy of the Bush administration, and attributed the administration's slow response to the fact that such a huge proportion of the victims were African American. It is entirely possible that this guide in North Korea was better informed about Hurricane Katrina than I was.

This experience led me to test how well informed other guides were. Despite all my off-the-wall questions, I have found only one subject that renders guides speechless—questions about life after Kim Jong-il. When I have asked guides at Mount Kumgang and in Pyongyang about Kim Jong-il's sons and who might take over once he dies—as I put it, "in the same way that Kim Jong-il succeeded Kim Il-sung"—I have been met first with silence and then with an angry response. "They are just an ordinary family, why are you asking about them?" snapped one guide at Mount Kumgang. A fierce female guide in Pyongyang was much more heated: "Don't ask those questions," she screeched as she stormed away from me. This reaction was illuminating to me. Kim Jong-il's successor appeared to be the one topic that the guides had not been prepared to address, the one subject that cannot be discussed in North Korea.

One of the questions I am asked most often about North Korea is how many "ordinary people" I get to speak to. The answer is none. In fact, I do not even really try anymore. On my first visit, in August 2005, I went for a walk and asked a woman selling apples from a cart how much the apples cost. She muttered the answer and shooed me away, her eyes darting around to see whether anyone had seen me talking to her. During the same walk, I spotted a North Korean–English dictionary (there are differences between the North and South Korean dialects) in the window of a street kiosk and approached to ask if I could buy it with euros. The woman looked terrified just to see me approach and was positively catatonic when I asked the question in my rudimentary Korean. These incidents showed me that I am unlikely to get any useful information from ordinary people, and that even attempting to do so could be putting those people in danger. Finding out the price of a kilogram of apples is not worth it to me if it means that an innocent apple seller will be called in for questioning over her conversation with a "foreign spy."

As for life outside Pyongyang, we must rely on a variety of other sources. Diplomats and humanitarian workers based in the capital are a vital resource, as they are permitted to travel around the country and can report on the dire situation outside the showcase. They describe, for example, the challenges facing people who live in the rusting industrial cities along the east coast. One medical worker with extensive emergency room experience told me that the conditions at a hospital in Hamheung, near the east coast, were so bad she vomited. Since the introduction of halfhearted economic reforms in 2002 and the scaling back of the public distribution system of food rationing, people in rural areas have increasingly been growing their own vegetables in small private plots. But residents of urban centers such as Kim Chaek, a small city on the east coast, have no appropriate land for this purpose. Instead, aid workers report, these city-dwellers have resorted to trying to grow pumpkins on the roofs of apartment buildings. These kinds of examples help illustrate the increasing social disparities that are emerging in North Korea.

In addition to organizations based inside North Korea, there are South Korea–based humanitarian agencies—such as Daily NK and Good Friends—that extensively report on conditions in the North. These agencies produce a huge amount of information about changes in North Korea, including reports about rioting or acts of civil disobedience in areas such as North Hamgyong province. But because the agencies are highly politicized—many are actively seeking regime change in the North—their information can be questionable. For example, after the flooding in July last year, Good Friends, a Buddhist organization, reported that as many as 55,000 people had been killed—a figure that was many times greater than the one humanitarian workers in Pyongyang were reporting and thus difficult to trust.

In Seoul, we also have a great resource in the thousands of North Korean refugees who have made it to the South. They are a valuable source of information about life inside North Korea, especially those new arrivals who have not yet absorbed the Southern mind-set—that is, they have not yet embraced a fast-paced capitalist lifestyle, with a focus on materialism and getting ahead. I have talked to these refugees extensively—about their lives in North Hamgyong province, the hardships of the mid-1990s famine, the repression they endured, their often traumatic escapes, the revelations of watching South Korean soap operas in China, and their treatment when they arrived in the South. While there is little that Western journalists can do to verify their reports, this kind of firsthand testimony is essential for our reporting.

There are, however, many caveats when it comes to using defector testimony. First, these days about 80 percent of refugees come from North Hamgyong province. This is where people considered least loyal to Kim Jong-il's regime are designated to live. North Korea operates on a kind of caste system of loyal, wavering, and hostile, according to which those perceived to be loyal may live in Pyongyang, and those perceived to be hostile are relegated to those parts of the country with the harshest conditions and the barest government assistance. North Hamgyong province is underdeveloped, oppressed, and backward even by North Korean standards, so the stories from its defectors offer a glimpse into only one part of North Korea. Second, the refugees soon discover that groups critical of North Korea seize on their stories, thereby motivating them to embellish their experiences as a way to better please their audience. This impulse is greatly exacerbated by a disturbing practice among some Japanese news organizations, that of paying refugees for their stories. Third, there is the problem of deliberate fabrication, due to the refugees' embarrassment about what they did in the North. I have interviewed at least one refugee who gave a fake occupation when recounting his time in the North because his real job was something more nefarious, involving the political police.

Despite all the pitfalls, refugee testimony forms a central piece of the North Korean jigsaw puzzle. Indeed, even refugees who have lived in the South for a longer period—many of them political escapees who held privileged positions in Pyongyang—can be a gold mine of information in their own way. One former Korean Central News Agency reporter bragged to me about how he knew more about South Korea than most South Koreans—and rattled off a list of port statistics to underline just how detailed North Korean monitoring of the South really is. While stories with obvious holes in them should be cut, I think accounts that ring true should be reported, albeit with a clear presentation of the caveats.

What We Choose to Write About

Without a doubt, the nuclear issue has defined recent coverage of North Korea. This is the story most relevant—rightly or wrongly—to global readers and the one of most critical concern to Washington. Given its rising circulation in the United States and its steady efforts to increase its coverage of Asia, the *Financial Times* has devoted significant space to the North Korea issue. Developments in this story regularly make it onto the front pages of our Asian and U.S. editions, and we regularly run long analytical pieces and opinion columns on our op-ed pages.

Although the political story attracts the most attention, I would say that interest in North Korea is two-dimensional, focusing on the country's geopolitical situation on the one hand and on its weirdness on the other. In my visits to North Korea, I have always sought out new developments to write about, such as the results of the 2002 economic reforms and the food situation. I have deliberately avoided dwelling on the strangeness of the place, although the oddities are of course so pervasive that sometimes they cannot be avoided. However, it is the stories about North Korea's idiosyncrasies that seem to resonate the most with readers. I received many more comments on a story I wrote about Kim Jong-il's January 2006 visit to Guangzhou—a lighthearted weekend read about the media shenanigans surrounding the Great Leader's whereabouts—than I did about a two-thousand-word piece analyzing how the U.S. freezing of North Korean deposits at the Banco Delta Asia had created more problems than it solved.

In addition, I have tried to concentrate on changes in the North Korean economy. I have written, for example, about factories I have visited, where the central authorities have devolved more responsibility to managers; about the establishment of the Pyongyang Business School; about sales in Pyongyang stores that suggest a new, un-Communist interest in making money; and about signs of merchant activity on the city's streets. The Kaesong industrial complex, on the northern side of the DMZ—which the South Korean government championed as a beacon of inter-Korean cooperation and which journalists can easily visit—has provided a window into North Korea's fitful economic changes. But, as with visits to Pyongyang, we must be aware that this is not the real North Korea. It is a very unique economic quarantine zone, a little slice of South Korea in the north, and is not replicated outside the Hyundai-supplied fences that surround it.

I have chosen to concentrate on the economy partly because it is one of the few areas where tangible change—for better or for worse—can been seen; partly because I write for the *Financial Times*, which focuses on economic issues; and partly because it is a way to differentiate my coverage from that of other journalists. Most of all, I have tried to show a bit of real life and to humanize North Korea. North Koreans crack jokes. They can be kind and hospitable. They are curious and get annoyed. North Koreans are people, too, and in my reporting I have tried to convey a sense that they should not be lumped together with Kim Jong-il and punished for the acts of a leader for whom they never voted in the first place. The Internet has facilitated this distinction by allowing us to write in the first person and to publish photo galleries, broadening the kind of coverage we can offer on North Korea.

During my first trip to Pyongyang, I wrote an online diary for the *Financial Times'* Web site, FT.com, which was much more interesting—to write and to read—than the usual "why North Koreans think they need nukes" stories (the latter invariably based on "interviews" with government-appointed hosts or tourist-site guides). In this diary I wrote about watching children splashing in public fountains on a hot day, drinking Daedonggang beer in a local pub where Korean men snacked on fried fish eyes, and being told by a doctor at a Pyongyang maternity hospital that I was welcome to give birth there when I decided to have children. I also wrote about my conversations with my guide, Mr. Ri, which covered everything from digital cameras and Tchaikovsky to the Michael Jackson trial and German ketchup. As Mr. Ri said to me one day: "People are people. Life is life." First-person accounts can help impart to readers a sense of what it is like to operate, if not live, in the most repressive of countries.

During that first visit, I was almost arrested after going for a walk near the Koryo Hotel in downtown Pyongyang and taking a few pictures along the way. I later learned that walking alone was permissible, and taking pictures with my guide was fine, but taking pictures alone was a crime tantamount to aggravated robbery. Within minutes I was accosted by a secret police officer who tried to confiscate my passport and who, together with a squad of other policemen who appeared from nowhere, proceeded to trail me around the streets when I refused to surrender my documents. The police were yelling at me, people were staring, and I was rattled—the entire situation seemed to me to exemplify the constraints of life in Pyongyang, albeit at the low end of the harassment scale.

I hoped that by writing about such events I could bring "my North Korea"—the highly sanitized, choreographed version of the country that I was allowed to see—to life in much more vivid detail than I could have if I had stuck to straight newspaper reporting. Certainly, I received much more feedback about the diary—which was published with dozens of photos I took in Pyongyang—than about any news story I wrote from that trip. I think I received such a strong response not only because writing an online diary allowed me to write in a more chatty, colorful way than I could in the newspaper but also because these experiences were new and enabled me to report on North Korea in a more engaging fashion.

The one arena in which I detect waning reader interest is human rights in North Korea. Everyone knows that North Korea has one of the worst human rights records in the world, but with atrocities happening all over the globe, it is difficult to make those in North Korea newsworthy. The regime is impervious to United Nations condemnation and damning reports from nongovernmental organizations, so writing about human rights there can seem futile, which in turn affects reader interest. The lack of fresh information about the situation inside North Korea also makes this story difficult to sell to editors, who typically respond: "Didn't we already know that they operate cruel labor camps?" Presenting human rights abuses as "news" can be exceptionally difficult.

This certainly does not mean that we should not cover human rights issues. I believe it is incumbent on those of us who have personally witnessed a sliver of North Korean repression or listened to defectors recount the horrors of their lives in prisons and labor camps to continue to highlight these issues. There is little evidence as yet that North Korea has taken any notice, but we must continue to shine the spotlight into these dark corners.

Challenges

Much of the North Korea story has a déjà vu feel about it. After the latest burst of interest in the denuclearization talks, reader (and editor) fatigue will no doubt kick in again. The challenge for correspondents writing about this secretive and potentially dangerous place is to produce stories that are both new and true. We are inundated with difficult-to-confirm reports of Kim Jong-il's declining health and riots in the northern provinces, but deciding *not* to write a story—that is, deciding that a story, however sensational, is too tenuous or difficult to confirm—can be just as important as deciding to write one. Our standards for verification should be just as high for stories about North Korea as they are for stories about other countries.

There are endless challenges and pitfalls in reporting from North Korea, but I think that transmitting what we see in that country—even if it is sanitized—is better than not going at all, provided we disclose the necessary caveats. In writing down our observations, we can add something to the pool of knowledge about this most mysterious place. Ironically, on the same day in April 2007 when I was rebuked by Lt. Col. Ri at Panmunjom, another military man gave me some advice that made sense in my world as well as in North Korea. "You mustn't write things just from listening," said Col. Kang Ho-sup, of the Korean People's Army, as we walked along the DMZ. "You must check the facts with your own eyes, write what you see, write the truth."

You know how difficult it is to understand the inner workings of North Korea. As the *New York Times* journalist Smith wrote recently, today's spy satellites can read newspaper print on the ground, but even they can hardly penetrate to North Korea's actual conditions. . . . Didn't Gregg, our ambassador in South Korea, refer to North Korea as "a black hole"?

—CIA director James Woolsey briefs President Bill Clinton in *Ryŏksa ŭi taeha* (1997), a North Korean propaganda novel[1]

ON THE MEDIA'S INDIFFERENCE
TO NORTH KOREAN IDEOLOGY

B. R. Myers

What would we do if we learned that our next-door neighbor had begun amassing guns and ammunition? After contacting the police, and being reminded of every American's right to bear arms, we would likely waste no time putting our house on the market. Then we would lie awake and ponder the same few questions: What does our neighbor plan to do? What is he teaching his family? How does the household see itself and the world around it? We would probably be far less curious about the caliber of the man's weapons than about what made him choose to stockpile them in the first place.

For some reason, however, Western journalists regard North Korea's ideology and official culture as interference—as an obstacle and not an aid to understanding the country. One could follow the nuclear crisis for years, watching CNN, say, or reading the *Washington Post*, and never find out what the North Koreans believe. One would probably learn more about Kim Jong-il's hairstyle and his taste in cognac.

This would be understandable if North Koreans were tight-lipped about their beliefs, but they are not. Granted, the regime has set up an entire Potemkin ideology—Juche by name—to make foreigners think the country is ruled in accordance with humanist commonplaces such as "Man is the master of all things." The Korean Central News Agency also puts out English-language editorials that are meant to confirm the sympathetic Western view of a misunderstood country seeking integration into the world community. But neither fluency in Korean nor extensive research is needed to dig deeper. Like all nationalists, the North Koreans are incapable of putting themselves in a foreigner's shoes, so they do not realize how much they give away whenever they sing their own praises. An outsider can gain insight into their worldview simply by reading the official biography of Kim Il-sung (which for forty years has been available in English translation), by studying the canonical paintings of the personality cult, or by taking a guided tour of Pyongyang.

In large part, this worldview represents the continuation of the ideology instilled into Korean intellectuals during the colonial era (1910–1945). To put things as simply as possible: the Japanese ushered the Koreans into the world's purest race, and in 1945 the Koreans ushered the Japanese out of it. Though the Koreans continued to regard themselves as uniquely virtuous thanks to a pure and ancient bloodline, that bloodline now became theirs alone. But whereas the "imperial" Japanese race viewed their bloodline as a protective talisman, the Koreans now believed their virtue had made them as vulnerable as children to an evil world. It was the new Parent Leader's mission to protect the child-race and lead it to its rightful place at the center of the world stage. This elementary and appealing perspective of "foreigners bad, Koreans good, Leader best"—a worldview incompatible with Marxism, Confucianism, *and* Juche thought—has always determined official policy. It is little wonder, then, that North Korea is incapable of maintaining fraternal relations even with its allies, that its personality cult resembles Hirohito's far more than the cults of Stalin and Mao, and that it has recently revived colonial-era kamikaze rhetoric.

Despite such abundant evidence to the contrary, journalists persist in describing North Korea as a Stalinist state. Most do so only in passing, with no attempt to explain the term. More often than not it is belied by the very phenomenon they are reporting on—the regime's effort to attract foreign investment, for example, or the practice of forcing pregnant returnees from China to undergo abortions. Journalists seem to use the label "Stalinist state" mainly for the sake of variation, much as entertainment correspondents use the epithet "the Material Girl" not to impute materialism to Madonna but simply to avoid repeating her name. Not long ago a reporter nonchalantly admitted as much to me: "Well, we can't be saying 'North Korea' all the time."

Only slightly less superficial is the press's treatment of the official pseudodoctrine. On the one hand, journalists naively swallow the official assertion that everything in North Korea revolves around Juche. On the other hand, they make no effort to explain its tenets. At most it is described as a mélange of "isms"—Marxism, nationalism, Confucianism, even shamanism—that somehow boils down to an obsession with "self-reliance," as *juche* (literally "subject") is usually mistranslated into English. This hardly sounds like Stalinism. Still less does it sound like North Korea, which since 1945 has depended more heavily on foreign aid than any other country in the region. Journalists' indifference to these obvious contradictions indicates that they do not really mean the word *juche* any more than they mean the word *Stalinist*. And yet the same people are very careful about how they report on the country's nuclear program or human rights abuses, refusing to assert anything that cannot be verified. It is as if the motivation for North Koreans' behavior were trivial in comparison with the behavior itself, and therefore undeserving of accurate reporting.

Of course, coverage of the Kim Jong-il regime is not unique in this respect. The media have, for example, perfected the extraordinary feat of discussing Islamism without discussing Islam. This neglect of ideology and culture is common to our society as a whole. Decades ago, when discussing the European Common Market, the British critic Ian Robinson wrote of "a failure to *see* [cultural differences] brought on by the modern Western prejudice that only economic management is real and that everything else follows from it."[2] Though Marxism has fallen out of fashion, this central fallacy of Marxism has never been more popular; to advocates of globalization it is an especially cherished article of faith. Islamic terrorism must therefore be attributed to economic deprivation, despite the enormous wealth of the men who bankroll it. The possibility that mere worldviews can lead to implacable conflict is one of the many unthinkables that now hem in journalism, academic research, and indeed all edited discourse in the United States.

But if the West shies away from taking a hard look at religion, it is even more reluctant to devote critical attention to foreign nationalisms, especially those of the blood-based sort. Western journalism usually misrepresents Korean nationalism as a millennia-old patriotism heightened by constant historical trauma. The reader will never find out that it is only about a hundred years old and owes an enormous debt to fascist Japanese thought. Nor will the reader learn of the Korean nationalist's belief in the *inherent* moral superiority of his race, because to report unequivocally on such things is to violate the rule that racism may be attributed only to white people.

Let me admit that I feel uneasy attributing racism to a people that has too often been on the receiving end of it. Alas, the only alternative word available in our language is "ethnocentricity," which does not do justice to the notion that Koreans are uniquely virtuous: capable of moral transgressions when under duress but never evil by nature.[3] This notion is common in both North *and* South, and even among those who have moved to other countries. Days after the massacre at Virginia Tech in 2007, a letter from a Korean American appeared in the *New York Times* expressing shock that a *Korean* could have done such a thing.[4] (I might add that the only gunman to have murdered more people in one spree was Woo Bom-kon in South Korea in 1982.)[5] No correspondent pursued this angle; reporting on cultural issues is fine if it highlights the charming variety of the global family, but not if it undermines the idea of such a family. I still believe that a serious discussion of Korean nationalism has a greater right to appear in the *New York Times* than the bemused coverage of Korean pop-culture curiosities that I find there so often.

Perhaps Western journalists are not conscious enough of the importance of North Korea's ideology to realize that they are failing to report significant truths. They evidently hold to the old-fashioned view that propaganda is cynically cooked up by elites who do not believe it themselves. More interest is shown in the offhand remarks that Kim Jong-il astutely drops in the presence of visiting diplomats. U.S. government officials fall for this, too. One of them responded to a lecture I had given on North Korean culture by saying, "Kim doesn't believe that nonsense himself; he told Madeleine Albright it's all fake." Western journalists and diplomats once responded in comparable fashion to Nazi propaganda, laughing it off as politically expedient bluster and telling everyone what a reasonable man Hitler really was.

Since World War II, however, observers like Jacques Ellul have convincingly argued that propaganda is not created from nothing but, like advertising, reflects myths and needs that were already there.[6] It therefore follows that Kim Jong-il is hardly less likely to believe his propaganda than are his subjects, and that by studying propaganda we can gain insight into the country as a whole. Indeed, the most convincing analysis of North Korea ever written was by an Austrian philosophy professor who simply paid close attention to the monuments, paintings, and performances that his guides wanted him to see.[7] Because people's needs change, propaganda also changes, in North Korea as in our own country.

Journalists, however, continue to regard Pyongyang's propaganda as monolithic, unchanging, predictable, and artificial—in short, as inherently *un*-newsworthy. To them it is a veil obscuring the interesting North Korea, the North Korea of economic and basic human needs. When a tour guide praises Kim Jong-il, journalists assume that he is mechanically "spouting the official line." Only when the guide talks of his own family life or touches on material hardship is he truly being himself, showing "the real North Korea." Rather than go to Kim Il-sung's birthplace or other official sites, journalists would prefer to visit a provincial supermarket for a look at the shelves, or an open-air market to gauge the price of rice. High on everyone's wish list is a visit to a private home, but here too the apparent motivation is to learn about living standards and not customs. Culture is of interest only when it appears to run counter to the ruling myths. The Western press hurried to tell us that children of the Workers' Party elite had started tinting their hair and using South Korean slang. And yet a sharp upswing in the party's anti-American propaganda during the arms negotiations of 2003—negotiations supposedly aimed at improving relations between Pyongyang and Washington—went unreported.

I do not mean to suggest that the media should ignore stories about North Korea's unofficial or "second society," to borrow a term coined by the sociologist Elemér Hankiss in regard to post-totalitarian Hungary.[8] The viewing of smuggled videos and DVDs, for example, is an important and potentially revolutionary development that deserves our attention. Nor do I want journalists to stop reporting on illicit markets, or on the malnutrition that continues to plague the populace. My quarrel is with the assumption that *only* North Korea's "second society" is worth writing about. To return to the analogy I made at the start of this chapter, it is as if, having been invited into our arms-collecting neighbor's home, we paid no attention to what he had to say, instead trying to peek into his fridge or catch his children in an unguarded moment. Perhaps the fallacy that North Korea is a Stalinist state encourages reporters to focus on the sort of unsanctioned activity that famously undermined the Eastern Bloc. But we know from defectors that North Korea's black-market vendors see their work as strengthening the country, and thus as a patriotic, Kim-affirming activity. We should also beware of equating a fondness for Western culture with a fondness for the West itself. (Some Pyongyang-watchers have even claimed that North Koreans' interest in learning English reflects a desire for better relations with Washington!)[9] This is wishful thinking of a kind to which Americans are especially prone. We should keep in mind that South Koreans have no difficulty reconciling a love of Japanese pop culture with an equally fervent hatred of

Japan. More to the point, the North Koreans were never more hostile to the Russians than when they were soaking up Soviet culture in the 1940s and 1950s.

When I talk to journalist friends who are based in Seoul, they express great interest in the North Korean worldview. When I ask why they don't write about it more often, they complain of editorial pressures, space constraints, and the public's presumed aversion to abstract issues. But it takes no more space to write "blood-based nationalism" (a self-explanatory term) than to pay lip service to the fallacies of "hard-line Stalinism" or "the Juche ideology of self-reliance." In my own experience of writing for American newspapers and magazines, I have found editors and readers alike to be much more interested in North Korean propaganda than in, say, the plight of lonely refugees in Seoul. Some journalists assume that the personality cult is old news because it has been around for sixty-odd years, but it has never received much serious attention. The cult of Kim Jong-il in particular is still terra incognita. Only a handful of experts are aware, for example, that he is not a "Confucian patriarch" but is instead often referred to as "mother."

Does this mean that journalists are extreme adherents of the orthodoxy that only economic issues really matter? No. My impression is that they feel a moral duty to "show the human side" of North Korea, to serve the cause of peace and understanding by revealing that people there have the same basic hopes and needs as we do. Although I understand this "humanizing" urge, it seems to me misguided, and not merely because readers do not want to read about sameness. A North Korean is just as human when he is bowing to a Kim Il-sung statue as when he is foraging for food. One might even argue that he is more human in the former activity, the latter one being common to animals as well. And far from advancing international peace by ignoring the distinguishing characteristics of the average North Korean's humanity—his adulation of Kim Il-sung, his belief in the moral superiority of his race, and so on—Western journalists are making a conflict more likely. Wars used to be fought under the assumption that foreigners were not human; now they are fought under the equally idiotic assumption that every human is basically the same. It was the *downplaying* of cultural differences by government and media alike that led Americans to expect a euphoric reception for U.S. troops in Iraq. Talking heads crowed in 2003 when Saddam's radio stations were "taken out." We were led to believe that once the propaganda machine fell silent, the locals would begin behaving like us, because who *doesn't* want democracy and prosperity? Had we paid more attention to what divides Iraqis and Americans, the tragic debacle might have been avoided.

I began this chapter with an excerpt from a propaganda novel that makes plenty of comic hay out of America's cluelessness. One can hardly blame the writer for laughing at us. As long as we ignore the blood-based nationalism that binds the regime to its people, North Korea will remain a "black hole" to America, and no number of articles or intelligence reports will ever add up to a truly informative picture of the country. One might as well try to make sense of Iran while mistaking it for a Buddhist republic. Though the North Koreans do indeed have many of the same needs and beliefs that we do, they also hold very different ones, and it is the journalist's duty to dwell more on the latter than the former. No one need fear that in realizing the implacability of the North's xenophobia, the American people will be more likely to endorse the use of military force against the country. On the contrary, far fewer Americans would support such action if they better understood the ideological landscape of the peninsula—if they understood, in other words, that U.S. troops are in effect protecting moderate Korean nationalists from radical Korean nationalists. A less sensible use of our power is hard to imagine.

Notes

[1] Chŏng Kijong, *Ryŏksa ŭi taeha* (Pyongyang: Munhakyesulchonghapch'ulp'ansa, 1997), 362. Translation mine.

[2] Ian Robinson, *The Survival of English* (London: Cambridge University Press, 1973), 116.

[3] C. Fred Alford explores the Koreans' refusal to attribute evil to one another in *Think No Evil: Korean Values in the Age of Globalization* (Ithaca, NY: Cornell University Press, 1999). Evidently unaware of how readily they attribute it to foreigners, Alford wrongly claims in his book's preface (p. x) that Koreans have no concept of evil at all.

[4] "When the news broke that the gunman was a 23-year-old Korean immigrant, I was in total shock. As a Korean-American, I never thought or imagined that this type of crime could be done by a Korean." (Letter to the editor, Christine Lee of Northvale, NJ, April 18, 2007, published in the *New York Times*, April 19, 2007.)

[5] "South Korean Shootings Lead Minister to Resign," *New York Times*, April 29, 1982.

[6] Jacques Ellul, *Propaganda: The Formation of Men's Attitudes* (New York: Vintage, 1975), 198–99.

[7] See Alfred Pfabigan, *Schlaflos in Pjöngjang* (Vienna: Verlag Christian Brandstätter, 1986).

[8] Elemér Hankiss, "The 'Second Society': Is There an Alternative Social Model Emerging in Contemporary Hungary?" *Social Research* 55, nos. 1–2 (1988), 13–42.

[9] David Kang, "We Should Not Fear the North Koreans," *Los Angeles Times*, June 13, 2000.

DECODING THE NORTH KOREAN ENIGMA

Caroline Gluck

D awn was breaking, and I was both nervous and excited as I prepared to do my first-ever live television interview with the BBC—a broadcast that would be watched by millions of viewers around the world. Television cameras stood on a hotel rooftop, spewing yards of cables and connectors. Behind my assigned position, early-morning traffic moved slowly along the main road.

But this wasn't the high-tech South Korean capital, Seoul, where I had been based for more than a year. In Seoul, high-speed broadband Internet and satellite news-gathering (SNG) trucks were the norm. This was decidedly low-tech North Korea—a country that curtails freedom of speech, where you can be jailed for listening to foreign media broadcasts, and where only the most senior officials are allowed Internet access. The country monitors foreign visitors carefully—requiring them to hand in any mobile phones when they arrive at the airport and to pick them up when they leave—and is suspicious of visits by foreign reporters.

I had come to the so-called Hermit Kingdom during a brief period when the state had been opening its doors, ever so slightly, to the outside world. The historic inter-Korean summit had taken place a year before, in 2000, sparking a flurry of inter-Korean exchanges, including emotional family reunions between people who had been separated for more than half a century.

The South was suddenly fascinated with all things North Korean. North Korean pop songs were in vogue, teenagers were buying sunglasses and clothes like those worn by North Korean leader Kim Jong-il, and television sets made in the North under a joint venture project went on sale in the South. The rest of the world showed a similar surge of interest in the reclusive country. People wanted to know more about what life was really like in this enigmatic nation, and what lay behind the stark headlines.

It was my first visit to the North Korean capital. I had arrived as part of a large media contingent—seventy-five foreign reporters in all, the largest group of journalists ever to travel to the North. We accompanied a troika from the European Union (EU): Chris Patten, European commissioner for external relations; Javier Solana, the EU's high representative for security and foreign affairs; and Swedish prime minister Göran Persson. At the time, Sweden held the six-month revolving EU presidency.

The stated goal of the visit was to increase the EU role in the inter-Korean peace process. Instead of just offering broad support to exchanges that had been initiated on the Korean Peninsula, the Europeans wanted to raise other key issues, such as economic reform, North Korea's missile program, human rights, humanitarian aid, and confidence-building measures. In the months after the inter-Korean summit, almost all EU member states and the European Commission had announced plans to establish formal diplomatic relations with North Korea.

But the visit took place at a sensitive time. Budding inter-Korean exchanges had come to a standstill after U.S. president George W. Bush angered North Korea by saying that his administration needed to review its policy before resuming dialogue with the totalitarian country. There were hopes that the EU visit to North Korea could provide some fresh impetus to the engagement policy that South Korea favored. The EU visit was regarded as a high-profile intervention in the peninsula, where American influence had traditionally predominated. As a result, there was huge interest in the visit. My editors had an enormous appetite for stories that would give the public better insight into North Korea, especially daily life in a country that was almost entirely reported as a policy and security issue.

At the airport, we were enthusiastically greeted by hundreds of cheering North Koreans, women wearing their traditional dress, *hanbok*, and waving bright pink plastic flowers—a reminder of the much larger but equally stage-managed reception that South Korean president Kim Dae-jung received when he arrived on his historic visit to the North in 2000. Once welcomed, we were herded onto buses and taken to the Koryo Hotel in downtown Pyongyang.

As journalists, we were eager to start reporting. The North Koreans divided us into groups, assigned us official minders and translators, and showed us to our rooms. They kept telling us to wait while closed-door meetings with officials took place. But we were getting agitated and impatient. We told our hosts that we had not traveled to North Korea to spend the day in the hotel: we needed to go somewhere, see something, and file something. The North Korean behavior was also clearly unsettling the normally calm Swedish officials traveling with us. Before our arrival, they had been given assurances that trips would be arranged for the media. They told their North Korean counterparts firmly that there was no way they could expect a group of nearly eighty reporters—all desperate to file a story—to stay put in the hotel.

Their insistence paid off. But the need for such pressure in the first place typified a pattern of communications with North Korean officials that I saw time and again on my reporting trips to the country. Warm welcomes and promises led to stonewalling, then to threats and counterthreats, which were followed by apparent breakthroughs. Reporting in North Korea was never easy or straightforward. On this trip, reporters were allowed to bring in satellite phones and other SNG equipment for broadcasting; such permission was often not granted on subsequent visits, and these denials, in turn, caused problems for future reporting trips. Problematic phone lines, for example, meant that it was hard to file anything more than the briefest news report or analytical comment. Even then, connections were so poor that BBC programs in London complained that the phone-line quality was unfit for broadcast. I once dialed London six times through hotel phone operators—there is no direct dialing in North Korea—trying to get a decent line, a task that took more than an hour.

My 2001 trip, like all trips to the North, was carefully choreographed. Notably, we had minders. No reporter ever comes to North Korea without at least one official assigned to look after him or her and to help translate (or, as we would complain, to keep tabs on us and prevent us from venturing out on our own). Often, the minders would try to treat us like tourists visiting the country. There would be obligatory visits to endless landmark sites—the Juche Tower, Kim Il-sung's mausoleum, various museums, and the International Friendship Exhibition at Mount Myohyang, a cavernous museum near Pyongyang, in which thousands of gifts given to the Great Leader and his son, Kim Jong-il, the current North Korean leader, are displayed. As for meeting the people themselves, North Korean defectors whom I had interviewed back in the South reminded me that when outsiders traveled anywhere in the country, most residents were warned to stay indoors until after the visitors had left. Aid workers, diplomats, and defectors also constantly told me that Pyongyang was not typical North Korea: it was the showcase capital where the elite and their families lived.

A chance to talk to "ordinary" people in the city, though, provided the richest insights. On this first visit, for example, we were shown Pyongyang's vast subway system and took a ride on the train. On the platform, pages of that day's newspapers were mounted on plastic notice boards, so that commuters could read them as they waited for the train. That day's paper was full of criticism of U.S. plans to build a national missile defense shield, which Washington had said was needed because of threats posed by states such as North Korea. One paper, the *Rodong Sinmun*—the organ of the North Korean Workers' Party—carried photographs of the EU delegation's visit.

It was here that I did my first "vox pop," as we refer to them in broadcasting: canvassing the person on the street, in this case a university teacher on the subway platform. Asking him what he thought about the EU visit, I got a carefully scripted reply that could have come from the mouth of a North Korean diplomat. He spoke of how Pyongyang wanted to develop good relations with "friendly" countries, why he considered the United States to be a hostile nation, and the reasons he believed that the EU, at this time, was on North Korea's side.

I was never entirely sure that even these seemingly spontaneous encounters were unplanned and unscheduled, offering a true window on the nature of society. My minders probably did not engineer the conversation with the man on the subway platform, but the fact that he was on the platform at the time foreigners were visiting was unlikely to be completely coincidental. He had probably been well briefed on what to say if questioned. Nothing is quite as it seems in North Korea.

Fortunately, even stage-managed events offered some glimpses into the tightly regulated lives of North Koreans and the thinking of the leadership. Showcase school visits revealed how the system of political indoctrination works. On one visit to a state-run nursery school during a later trip, I discovered the extent to which North Koreans receive a cradle-to-grave political education. There, children as young as two were being taught and quizzed about the country's leaders.

A few occasions, though, did yield spontaneous encounters. For example, while driving to the countryside on a later visit, we saw a group of "volunteers" working on a Sunday to build dykes next to the road. On our way back, I asked the North Koreans to stop the car. I got out and talked to a group of workers who told me they were volunteering their labor on what should have been a day of rest because they were determined to make their country stronger and better.

In North Korea, conversations with people are constantly filtered and translated through our assigned minders. I would always carefully check translations when I returned to Seoul. Unguarded comments that might have been made and detected, had I possessed the language skills to communicate directly with people, could offer new insights—or was this simply wishful thinking on my part? Indeed, South Korean journalists who visit the North often return complaining of the same restrictions and difficulties faced by Western reporters. All North Koreans know the consequences of speaking out against the regime.

Some cracks appeared in the system as a result of famine in the 1990s and widespread food shortages. These calamities forced people to travel from their home provinces in search of sustenance, sometimes to China. The population's sudden mobility undermined the state's tight system of control and exposed many North Koreans to information and news that were rigidly censored in their own country. But it was clear that, at home, the leadership still ran the show.

All of these obstacles notwithstanding, my early reporting trips to the North—however brief—were valuable. They gave me a better understanding of the country and its people and allowed me to write some stories that humanized a place otherwise so starkly portrayed in media reports. Until the 2000 summit, most news coverage of the North did not progress beyond the headlines: the famine, the nuclear threat, the North's military buildup, and sometimes shocking human rights stories based on interviews with recent North Korean defectors or nongovernmental lobby groups.

My visits provided contact, however choreographed, with North Korean citizens also gave me the chance to talk to aid workers and diplomats, many of whom, although they were wary of being officially quoted in our reports lest their operations be jeopardized, willingly gave off-the-record briefings. Such information was helpful later when I or my colleagues needed to confirm single-source reports coming out of the North.

On my first trip to Pyongyang, I was simply happy to be in the North and to report on what we were allowed to see. A newcomer to the capital, I was content to go anywhere. Everything was new and offered interesting insights for news coverage and analysis. On subsequent trips, I was under more pressure to return with news or features that added to the public's sum knowledge of what kind of place North Korea was and how its citizens lived. Ironically, I felt that the more often I visited, the larger more likely it was that I would not be able to glean any new information.

As a broadcaster, I faced other challenges. What would I be allowed to film? Officials were touchy about cameras being pointed toward certain people and places, particularly anything to do with the military. Unlike print journalists, who could later talk to analysts and flesh out reports with descriptions and personal reflections, I needed "real people" and "real voices" to illustrate a feature. More specifically, I required at least three different voices per radio package.

Every time I traveled to North Korea after my first visit in 2001, I submitted a wish list of places I wanted to visit for feature stories I had researched prior to my arrival. These lists would optimistically (if unrealistically) range from requests for an interview with Kim Jong-il and a visit to the nuclear facility at Yongbyon to more practical and less controversial but, it proved, equally difficult-to-arrange visits: to a collective farm, a church, the national film studio, and even the state-run news agency, KCNA.

Every visit, at some point, would end up in a battle with the minders. I was always pushing for more access; they preferred that I stick to the tourist sites. I tried to use the argument that they should use the opportunity of foreign media visits to tell the world their viewpoint, to show us a side of the country that rarely gets told, as they often complained about negative foreign reporting. Privately, perhaps, my minders might have accepted that argument, but it was unlikely to persuade higher-up officials to grant many of my requests. Even trying to report on largely noncontroversial issues was an uphill struggle.

Once in a while, however, my visits yielded unexpected results. In August 2001, I traveled to the North with a delegation of British businessmen who were investigating potential investment opportunities. Just days before I arrived, I had read reports of serious flooding along the east coast. When I arrived in Pyongyang, I rang a contact with the humanitarian office of the United Nations, who told me that they were traveling to the affected province the following day. They were willing to take me but said I would have to get approval from officials in charge of my visit. I was not surprised when my minder rejected this request. Aid workers had told me before that they normally had to give two to three days' notice in order to get official approval for visits outside the capital. Nevertheless, my minder told me that she would see what could be arranged separately for me—maybe later in the week.

Every day, I asked about the progress of my request. I was deeply skeptical of any breakthrough. But to my great astonishment, I was suddenly told that my request had been approved and we would travel the next day, a Friday. That was particularly unusual, as aid workers in the North had told me Friday was normally considered a "no contact with foreigners" day—a time when officials tried to limit all outside contact in order to dedicate themselves to political study or community work.

This trip offered some interesting insights. Especially strong was my impression—reinforced later by talking to aid workers who had traveled around the country—of how different things were out in the provinces, far away from the showcase capital. Some of these workers noted that local governments in several provinces, left to fend for themselves in feeding and caring for their populations, felt resentment toward Pyongyang. In the capital, officials had told me I could travel only to a specific location and talk to particular officials there. But when I arrived in Kangwon Province, officials there told me they were willing to offer me all the necessary help I needed and asked me: Where did I want to go? What did I want to see? Whom did I want to talk to? I was amazed. They recognized that, as a member of the international media promising to broadcast news of the flood impact, I could prove extremely helpful in their struggle to secure more aid for the region.

The only obstacle I faced was an occasion when my minders intervened as I was filming villagers who were trying to salvage rice and clean up their devastated villages. Soldiers were among those helping. As soon as I pointed my camera toward soldiers in military trucks who were taking part in the rescue and relief operation, there were alarmed cries of "No!" and hands across my camera lens, blocking my attempts to film. Nonetheless, it was a headline news story when I finally got back to Seoul and filed my television report via a satellite feed. My unscheduled Kangwon trip was a rare opportunity for a staff reporter to file a developing news story in the North firsthand. On my previous trips to the North, I had been trying to present another side of the country and its people, largely through features, rather than breaking news.

One of my most productive visits was a weeklong stay in December 2001, during which I traveled to a collective farm. The journey took us deep into the North Korean countryside on a day when snow was calf-deep and temperatures were well below freezing. At this time of year, the contrast between the capital and the rest of the country was stark. In Pyongyang, people wore thick padded jackets, wool hats, and leather shoes or boots. In the countryside, they were walking in the snow in simple canvas shoes, hardly any protection against the subzero temperatures. We passed houses with thin bamboo mats instead of glass in the windows. The further we drove, the more depressing the landscape became.

When we arrived at the farm, the cooperative leader briefed me on facts and figures and how many times the leadership had visited. Eventually, I asked if I could now visit the rest of the farm, to see people at work. "Oh, they're all out," came the reply. Having just been told that more than twelve hundred families lived on the farm, I reacted with incredulity and tried not to lose my temper. After such a long drive in atrocious weather, I made it clear I would not leave without seeing more of the farm beyond the room in which we had gathered for tea. Inexplicably, appropriate individuals were "found," and I began a tour. In the end, I was quite excited to be told I could visit a family flat, a privilege rarely given to outsiders. I chatted to a clearly nervous family about how they lived. Tiny details—how they kept chickens in the kitchen during the winter and what they could grow in their small vegetable garden—all built for me a unique picture of their lives.

Another day, I visited a state-sanctioned Protestant church in Pyongyang. I was filming, hoping I would have enough footage to make a report about religion in the North. There had been consistent reports from church and human rights groups about widespread restrictions on religious freedom. However stage-managed the service was, it was nonetheless a rare opportunity and provided some great television footage. I was also fortunate to meet some visiting South Korean Christian groups; I contacted them for follow-up interviews back in Seoul, where they could chat more freely.

There was an ironic moment when my minder on this trip helped me film my piece. She made sure I was clearly framed and pressed the "record" button on my video camera as I talked about reported crackdowns against members of underground churches in the North and those who had had contact with foreign missionaries. I half expected her to interrupt my comments and complain. But no, she merely asked me to review what we had filmed and check if it was OK. North Korea can be full of surprises.

Throughout my stay in Seoul, North Korea and its budding—and then deteriorating—relations with the South and the United States was a big international news story. I never had an editor turn down a story pitch; such was the appetite for news about the North. From the historic North-South summit in 2000 and moving accounts of families separated for fifty years by the division of the peninsula to coverage of Kim Jong-il as a global security threat and serial human rights abuser, North Korea was considered priority news. Even softer feature stories were eagerly received, since they were considered pieces of a larger jigsaw puzzle that might offer some explanation of the North Korean enigma.

For journalists, North Korea restricted our access and often exasperated and perturbed us with its sometimes contradictory and often inexplicable behavior. But by allowing foreign reporters in at all, I believe the country has made itself less of an enigma and more a place that the public can "read"—and perhaps even relate to.

ADVENTURES IN THE "AXIS OF EVIL"

Barbara Slavin

During the first North Korean nuclear crisis, in 1993, I was home taking care of my young son and frankly did not give the story much attention. When I joined *USA Today* in 1996, I was drawn to the country by a different crisis—reports that tens of thousands of North Koreans were starving to death, due to the end of Cold War assistance from other Communist countries and decades of economic mismanagement.

Hoping to provide the first Western report on the famine, I began contacting anyone who might persuade the North Koreans to give me a visa. My employers encouraged me as I made the rounds of North Korean diplomats at the United Nations (UN) and representatives of UN agencies with staff in North Korea. I spoke to the handful of Americans who had traveled to the country, including Korean Americans and heads of charitable organizations, and finally struck gold with Congressman Tony Hall, an Ohio Democrat who chaired a humanitarian caucus in the House of Representatives. In April 1997 the North Koreans gave me permission to accompany Hall on a five-person congressional delegation (CODEL) for the purpose of fact-finding. I was listed as the "official rapporteur" for the CODEL, but everyone knew I was going as a newspaper reporter. The Clinton administration facilitated the trip by allowing me to fly to Pyongyang on a U.S. military plane from a U.S. airbase in Japan.

We spent only five days in North Korea, but the trip remains among the most moving and memorable experiences I have had as a journalist and underlies my continuing interest in the country. Desperate for aid and trusting Hall not to exploit their plight for propaganda purposes, the North Koreans allowed us to travel from Pyongyang to Sinuiju, on the Yalu River, in a convoy of Mercedes Benzes. Hall was permitted to bring along a Korean-speaking American translator and to stop the convoy anywhere he wanted. I was allowed to interview what seemed to be ordinary people (in North Korea, even "spontaneous" events may have some element of staging) and take roll after roll of pictures.

More than the story I subsequently wrote for *USA Today*, those pictures dramatized North Korea's plight. The paper printed an entire page of images that showed people pulling tractors like human oxen, hillsides denuded of trees, young girls and old women scavenging for weeds, and hungry babies crying in an orphanage. Some of the pictures were used by Korean American organizations to support a drive for contributions for food aid. A State Department official told me later that the photos helped prompt the administration to allocate an additional $3 million in U.S. assistance to North Korea that year. The pictures still resonate. I was amazed not long ago to find one of them—of an old woman holding an empty pot—on the cover of a Refugees International report. Among the interviews I conducted on that trip, the one that stays with me most was with a young man, Kim Gyong-il, at a hospital in Sinuiju. Hollow-cheeked from hunger and suffering terrible stomach pains from eating sawdust, he told me: "The Americans started the war in Korea. But if you help us with our food troubles, you will be most welcome."

I got another remarkable glimpse of North Korea in the fall of 1997, thanks to the Pentagon's efforts to recover the remains of more than eight thousand Americans listed as missing in action (MIA) since the Korean War. Along with representatives of several U.S. veterans' groups and a reporter and crew from CBS, I drove deep inside the country to Unsan, a hundred miles north of Pyongyang. We watched a team of eight Americans working alongside sixty North Korean soldiers digging for G.I. remains in rugged terrain that resembled Appalachia. They showed us rusted remnants of cans of C-rations, grenades, and other detritus from a war that killed up to four million people, including fifty-four thousand Americans. We stayed in a threadbare 1960s-era mountain resort that housed more cockroaches than humans. We were treated to a banquet in a tent in the mountains where a macho North Korean Army colonel named Pak tried to get me drunk on snake wine. He failed but seemed to have fun trying.

At the time, both the Clinton administration and the North Koreans hoped these humanitarian contacts would smooth the way for the restoration of diplomatic relations, much as similar activities had softened U.S.-Vietnamese enmity. The MIA missions continued until 2005 and resulted in the recovery of more than 220 sets of remains. At that point, then secretary of defense Donald Rumsfeld canceled the program, complaining of problems in communicating with the U.S. teams inside North Korea and North Korea's refusal to return to the Six-Party Talks on its nuclear program.

I was fortunate to have had this on-the-ground experience before I turned to reporting on the nuclear proliferation issue. These early trips helped me to understand the North Koreans' mentality, their sense of vulnerability, and their ferocious bargaining skills. The visits also provided contacts with a handful of North Korean officials who proved useful for other stories, and made it easier for me to cultivate sources among American, South Korean, and Japanese diplomats, many of whom had never been to North Korea and wanted to talk to someone who had. Prior experience as a student in the Soviet Union in the 1970s and as a young reporter in China in the early 1980s helped me to see North Korea in context, as a member—albeit an extremely eccentric one—of a shrinking socialist community.

My coverage turned from humanitarian to military matters after the North Koreans tested a missile that overflew Japan in 1998. Rumsfeld, who was a drug company executive at that time, led the Team B assessment (alternative study) that accused the CIA of underestimating the spread of ballistic missiles. The Republican-led Congress began threatening to cut off the fuel-oil funds for North Korea promised under the 1994 Agreed Framework. William J. Perry, the secretary of defense under Bill Clinton, chaired a committee that presented new policy options, among them greater engagement. The Clinton administration took Perry's advice and invited a senior North Korean official to Washington in 2000. Madeleine Albright accepted a reciprocal invitation to North Korea in October 2000.

I was among the dozen or so reporters who accompanied Albright and was extremely fortunate to be a pool reporter in the room when Albright met with North Korean leader Kim Jong-il. Both wore high heels and were about the same height. I was only six feet away from them, and the hairs on the back of my neck stood up when they shook hands in front of a magenta-tinged mural on a chartreuse rug. Even without the neon colors, it would have been a dramatic scene. The next day, the official *Rodong Shimbun* newspaper published a huge front-page photograph of the meeting, which showed Kim and his officials next to Albright and her entourage. The message appeared to be that the long enmity between the two countries was over. I thought the fact that Albright and so many of her senior aides were women also sent a slyly subversive signal in a land of unreconstructed male chauvinists.

Albright took a lot of flack back home for dancing to music at a kindergarten during her stay. She was also criticized for attending a performance of North Korea's famous synchronized card turners. On important political anniversaries, these performers put on shows that combine the fascist flavor of a Nazi military parade with the acrobatic flair of a Super Bowl halftime show. Albright had been scheduled to go to the circus instead, but the North Koreans switched the program at the last minute, and it would have been an insult to her hosts had she refused to go.

During this visit, I was struck by the changes that had taken place since my 1997 trips. Emulating the Chinese of two decades earlier, the North Koreans had opened stores that took only hard currency, and restaurants that catered to foreigners and privileged North Koreans. The waitress in a Japanese restaurant in Pyongyang accepted tips—a sort of spiritual pollution previously unheard of in North Korea. There were a few more cars on the streets of Pyongyang and many more bicycles. My colleagues in the U.S. press corps devoted many column inches to how dreary things were, unaware that the situation, at least in the capital, appeared marginally better than in the past.

My newspaper fully supported these trips. North Korea was exotic and bizarre and visas were hard to come by. In the view of my editors, any visit there was newsworthy. That editorial interest continued even after the Clinton administration departed and the Bush administration began to move away from engagement. *USA Today*'s front page featured the rift between the Koreas that emerged in March 2001, when then secretary of state Colin Powell was obliged to retract his comment that the Bush administration would "pick up where Clinton left off" on talks with North Korea over missiles. The story took on larger significance as the first concrete example of the ongoing conflict between State Department pragmatists and White House/Pentagon ideologues. In the first

Bush term, the ideologues kept winning and U.S.-Korean relations continued to deteriorate. The second nuclear crisis began in October 2002, when the story broke that the North Koreans had admitted to seeking another route to nuclear weapons through uranium enrichment.

That story was a scoop I shared with Chris Nelson of the *Nelson Report,* who has also contributed a chapter to this book. Chris tells me he did not publish his piece, at the urging of U.S. officials. I have been asked many times by South Korean reporters how I got the story. It did not come from the Bush administration or from hardliners outside the government. At the time, the administration was trying to convince Congress to authorize the invasion of Iraq, and it wanted no distractions from any other rogue state, particularly on the weapons of mass destruction (WMD) front. Meanwhile, U.S. diplomats, hoping to preserve some relationship with North Korea, wanted breathing space to figure out how to contain the damage.

Had the White House chosen to leak the story, I probably would not have been the recipient, not only because I am a State Department reporter but because my prior reporting from North Korea would have suggested that I might have a more nuanced view of the country than members of the press who have not covered it firsthand. My source for the scoop was a former administration official who had heard, secondhand, about a North Korean's admission to Jim Kelly, then assistant secretary of state. The State Department spokesman at the time, Richard Boucher, told me I was onto something but refused on-the-record confirmation for a day. That delay gave the White House time to try to minimize the damage by giving the story to my competitors at an 8 p.m. briefing the day before we were to publish. (David E. Sanger of the *New York Times*, who also contributed a chapter to this book, informs me that he knew earlier in the day and received independent confirmation a few hours before the briefing.) From a press management perspective, giving a scoop to other papers is an attempt to get all the bad press out at once and to avoid having a story become a two- or three-day sensation as other papers try to match the original story.

Subsequently, administration officials who had long opposed the 1994 Agreed Framework worked, successfully, to bury it. They did so by broadly leaking information that suggested North Korea had not only set up an entire uranium enrichment plant but was also moving swiftly to build bombs from highly enriched uranium. It is instructive to look back at stories we wrote at the time. One piece I cowrote with *USA Today*'s then White House correspondent, Larry McQuillan, published October 18, 2002, begins: "The Bush administration believes that North Korea could be as little as one year away from being able to mass produce nuclear weapons." It continues: "A senior administration official said the North Koreans had been working on producing weapons-grade uranium for several years. U.S. intelligence thought the program was merely research and development. . . . But this summer, North Korea began a large-scale acquisition of materials for a gas centrifuge. . . . The official said there was no question what the North Koreans are up to. U.S. intelligence does not know where the facility is located. Materials for the plant are believed to have come from Pakistan and Russia."[1]

My colleagues wrote similarly alarmist pieces and presumably had the same sources—hardliners in the White House and the State Department whose surnames begin with "J" and "B," respectively. Amid the uproar, the administration cut off the fuel-oil deliveries to North Korea promised under the Agreed Framework. North Korea responded by kicking out arms inspectors, withdrawing from the Nuclear Non-Proliferation Treaty, and resuming production of plutonium. In 2003 I cowrote a story with a colleague, John Diamond, which basically said that the October 18, 2002, story was bunk. The lead was: "A year after North Korea provoked a crisis with the United States by admitting a secret effort to make weapons-grade uranium, U.S. officials say the program appears to be far less advanced than diplomats had feared. . . . A U.S. intelligence official says the CIA, which has conducted extensive surveillance of North Korea, is not certain there even is a uranium enrichment plant."[2] The October 18, 2002, story ran on page 1, as did my solo scoop saying that North Korea had admitted to having a uranium program. The story I wrote with John Diamond in 2003 ran on page 18A. The second, solo story attracted renewed notice in March 2007, when I reminded Chris Nelson about it. He reprinted it in the Nelson Report to show that a more recent "scoop" by David E. Sanger was, in many respects, four years old. The Sanger piece reported that the U.S. intelligence community had changed its assessment of the uranium program from "high" confidence to "moderate" confidence. Sanger's story also reflected administration efforts to defend the decision to sign a new nuclear agreement with the North Koreans, in the face of harsh criticism by former U.S. officials (J and B, again) who had opposed such negotiations.[3]

In my paper, the North Korea story began slipping off the front page after the collapse of the Agreed Framework. The Bush administration refused to label the situation a crisis and my editors seemed to agree. Colin Powell provoked much laughter among the press corps at a news conference in Beijing in early 2003 when he forgot his instructions for a moment and said that the United States sought "a peaceful and diplomatic solution to the crisis." He paused and then quickly rephrased: "a peaceful and diplomatic solution to the situation that currently exists between the international community and North Korea." Jim Kelly, appearing before a House committee a week before Powell spoke, explained the administration's aversion to the "C-word." "When you have a crisis," he said, "that suggests that something needs to be done almost immediately."

Far from doing anything immediately, the Bush administration, absorbed by Iraq, took its time tending to the Korea "situation." The three-party, then six-party, diplomatic process that emerged to fill the vacuum left by the prolonged U.S. refusal to directly engage North Korea did not provide a compelling story for our readers. And North Korea's reluctance to allow U.S. reporters access to cover the situation within the country made it difficult to attract interest, especially as other foreign policy issues came to the fore.

North Korea's provocative missile and nuclear tests in 2006 did make the front page. What did not make the front page, at least in my paper, was the country's February 13, 2007, agreement to trade its nuclear program for energy aid and other diplomatic and economic concessions. The Banco Delta Asia story—in which the U.S. Treasury ruled against a Macau-based bank for complicity in illicit North Korean activities—also failed to get much attention. My editors were interested in printing that story only if I could find out first whether efforts to return North Korea's frozen $25 million had succeeded or failed. The *Wall Street Journal* was the first to report that a Russian bank had agreed to take the money.[4]

In my view, and based on the experiences I have had as a diplomatic correspondent, the mainstream American press faces two significant challenges in covering North Korea. First, the North Korea story faces huge competition from other, more menacing foreign policy problems, particularly its comrades in the so-called axis of evil, Iraq and Iran. Americans are understandably more focused on the fate of U.S. troops under fire in Iraq and on Iran's potential to develop nuclear weapons. North Korea has no known links with Islamic terrorism, the major issue for current U.S. foreign policy, nor has it deliberately killed any Americans for at least three decades (since an incident in the DMZ that resulted in the death of two U.S. soldiers). Overall, to the extent they think about North Korea at all, most Americans seem to have accepted it as a nuclear power. They believe that China will prevent North Korea from escalating military tensions and that the country will move slowly toward accommodation with South Korea, Japan, and the United States.

The second major challenge for U.S. reporters is access. I have tried periodically—and unsuccessfuly—for nearly a decade to get a visa to return to North Korea. I would like to see what has happened in the country since 2000 and believe that there have been newsworthy changes, perhaps some for the better. But without a visa, it is impossible to know and to report on developments. The lack of access is the fault of the North Koreans, first and foremost, but it also reflects the deterioration of U.S.–North Korea relations. It is very difficult for U.S. reporters to enter North Korea unless they are part of an official delegation, and such delegations have been virtually nonexistent since 2002. Chris Hill, who replaced Jim Kelly in 2005, has now visited North Korea several times, but access for U.S. journalists has not improved.

In the absence of firsthand reporting, I have relied on secondhand sources to gauge conditions in North Korea. Inevitably, that raises the question of bias. Americans who travel to North Korea regularly, including those who work for nongovernmental organizations, do not want to jeopardize that access by being too critical of the government. Those who have never visited the country may not want to spoil their chances of going or may be overly harsh out of irritation that they have not been able to visit. An entire cottage industry has grown up around defectors and human rights advocates who may have other agendas in dramatizing the genuine plight of refugees or of North Koreans still within the country. Prior to the 1997 election of Kim Dae-jung, South Korean diplomats tended to be overly critical of North Korea; the reverse has been true since the advent of Kim's sunshine policy toward the North. The South Korean press has often been overly optimistic about prospects for breakthroughs in North Korean behavior and in relations between Washington and Pyongyang. But it has also been helpful in documenting issues such as increasing Chinese investment in North Korea. With respect to sources, Japanese officials remain influenced by the scandalous North Korean abductions of Japanese citizens two decades ago. Chinese sources are among the most well informed, due to the growing Chinese business contacts with the North Koreans. But both are difficult for U.S.-based journalists to contact.

The politics of North Korea remain incredibly opaque. Kim Jong-il is seen in the United States, and in much of the rest of the world, as a tabloid figure, an eccentric maniac like the puppet who portrayed him a few years ago in a Hollywood movie, *Team America*. That impression will not change until a Western journalist is allowed to interview him—but so far he has refused all requests, even from the formidable Diane Sawyer. Reporters from other Western countries have had only limited access to North Korea, especially outside Pyongyang. So far, then, a fictional work by a former U.S. official, *The Corpse in the Koryŏ*, probably provides the best sense of what life in North Korea is really like.[5]

Notes

[1] Barbara Slavin and Larry McQuillan, "North Korea Hastens Nuclear Program," *USA Today*, October 18, 2002, 1.

[2] Barbara Slavin and John Diamond, "N. Korean Nuclear Efforts Looking Less Threatening," *USA Today*, November 5, 2003, 18A.

[3] See Chris Nelson, *The Nelson Report*, March 1, 2007; and David E. Sanger and William E. Broad, "U.S. Had Doubts on North Korean Uranium Drive," *New York Times*, March 1, 2007, 1.

[4] Jay Solomon and Gregory L. White, "Russia to Move North Korea Funds—U.S. Hopes Resolution Resumes Stalled Talks on Nuclear Program," *Wall Street Journal*, June 11, 2007.

[5] James Church, *The Corpse in the Koryŏ* (New York: St. Martin's Minotaur, 2006).

COVERING NORTH KOREA'S
NUCLEAR PROGRAM:
A VERY DIFFERENT WMD PROBLEM

David E. Sanger

In the immediate aftermath of the invasion of Iraq, Americans learned to their dismay how political agendas can taint both the assessment of and public declarations about a hostile nation's nuclear ambitions. Almost everything that the Bush administration claimed about Saddam Hussein's programs for weapons of mass destruction (WMD) turned out to be based on extrapolation, spin, or, in a few cases, fabrication. America's loss of credibility has been huge. President Bush admitted that it was difficult for him to make a public case about American intelligence findings concerning Iran—and, presumably, other nations. Yet when he attempted to do so and it was reported in the press, the inevitable refrain went up: It's Iraq all over again, and once again the American media were cheerleading for war.

Historians of proliferation know that Iraq was something of an anomaly. Intelligence, and news reporting, about preparations to obtain and test nuclear weapons has often been inaccurate, but usually it has missed the boat in the other direction, by failing to capture accurately the progress that nations have made toward going nuclear. To varying degrees, underestimation of what was happening underground or behind closed laboratory doors led to similar misjudgments about the Soviet Union in the 1940s, China in the 1960s, India in the 1970s, Pakistan in the 1980s and 1990s, and Iraq before the Gulf War. Most important, it was years before the intelligence community, and reporters who cover proliferation, understood the scope of activities involving Abdul Qadeer Khan, the Pakistani engineer whose network dealt with North Korea, Libya, Iran, and perhaps countries we have yet to identify.

In that constellation, there is no example more journalistically complex or politically fraught than the strange case of North Korea. Ever since the armistice that ended, but never settled, the Korean War, there has been a lurking fear that some event could rekindle a five-decade-old conflict. The nuclear program seems a likely candidate. North Korea's slow, lurching progress toward amassing a nuclear arsenal has been under way for four decades. But not until the late 1980s did journalists for major news media begin writing in detail about the Yongbyon nuclear site, where much of the North's activity has been centered.

Since that time, the coverage has veered from urgent crisis—most notably in 1994, when the United States and North Korea came closer to conflict than at any time since the Korean War, and again after the country's nuclear test in 2006—to what could be best described as atomic ennui.

President George W. Bush declared that the United States would never "tolerate" a nuclear North Korea, but that is exactly what has happened since his father served in office. Public rhetoric aside, the United States has relied on conventional containment to make sure that the North's arsenal, however large or small, is never utilized. In the early 1990s the CIA estimated that the North had harvested enough nuclear material for one or two bombs. Despite this startling assessment, there was no journalistic inquest into who "lost Korea" to the nuclear club. Clearly, the threat was judged manageable, and the story was overshadowed by the Gulf War and the end of the Cold War.

In the years that followed, governments have inflated or deflated their assessment of that threat to fit specific agendas. When he served as president of South Korea, Kim Young-sam used to call reporters into the Blue House to criticize the United States for not taking the problem seriously enough. Then, when the temperature rose too high, he would summon them to complain that Washington was exaggerating the problem and itching for a fight; he would counsel patience.

In Washington, the Clinton administration tried hard to conceal its own internal debates in 1994 about whether to strike Yongbyon if the North moved its stockpile of fuel rods and began making bomb fuel. Only years later was it revealed that Defense Secretary William Perry was ready to threaten such action, though it has always been unclear whether President Clinton would have authorized him to follow through with it.[1]

In 2003 spin management of the intelligence reached a new level. The American news media have been castigated—sometimes rightly, sometimes unfairly—for "enabling" the war in Iraq by failing to express enough skepticism that Saddam Hussein had reconstituted his WMD. But the impassioned critique may miss a far deeper indictment: the press corps followed President Bush's lead so slavishly that journalists failed to pay sufficient attention to the speed with which North Korea and Iran were racing ahead with their nuclear programs, capitalizing on America's distraction in a war half a world away.

This problem was not universal. Several news organizations have invested heavily in understanding the nuclear programs in North Korea and, in recent years, Iran. But in early 2003 it is fair to say that much of the American media looked for WMD in all the wrong places. Reporters quickly learned that it was easy to sustain front-page or top-of-the-evening-news coverage about the suspected weapons programs of a nation the president was discussing daily. At the time, North Korea was expanding its nuclear arsenal at a pace that Saddam could only dream about. Yet precisely because the president wanted to focus American attention elsewhere, journalists found it extremely difficult to spark much interest in the strategic implications of a North Korea with eight or more weapons.

The logical contradiction was obvious. In North Korea and Iraq, America had two longtime enemies, both run by unpredictable dictators, both suffering from such large economic problems that their conventional military forces had withered. Both were so closed off to scrutiny—North Korea more than Iraq—that intelligence about their capabilities and intentions was poor at best. In the nuclear sweepstakes, North Korea was clearly far ahead of Iraq. But American public attention could not be focused on two major problems at once, and with U.S. forces flowing toward Iraq, and invasion obviously imminent, that story took the spotlight. The resulting media coverage was a classic example of what happens when America's journalistic agenda is too beholden to coverage of Washington's crisis du jour—a diabolical mixture of leaked intelligence information, politics, and very different perceptions of threats.

For journalists, the lessons of Iraq raise new and complex issues about proliferation reporting. As Iraq has demonstrated, reportorial skepticism about WMD intelligence is crucial. It is equally important to understand the dangers of missing critical turning points for nations seeking arms, particularly as reporters wrestle with covering the disarmament deal with the North and the growing confrontation with Iran. In both cases, intelligence may be played down or inflated to fit the administration's agenda. Maintaining journalistic balance—assessing the intelligence accurately, avoiding hype, analyzing the intentions of isolated dictators, and yet also forcing officials to confront intelligence they may not want to talk about—is a formidable enough task in ordinary times. The past few years have been extraordinary.

January 2003: The Bomb Washington Wanted to Ignore

In January 2003 all of Washington was focused on Iraq. American forces were flowing to Kuwait in anticipation of what appeared to be a forthcoming invasion. The media, both print and electronic, were captivated by Saddam Hussein's effort to account for his weapons stocks to the United Nations (UN), by the planning already under way for the postwar period, and by the United States' attempt to get its reluctant European and Asian allies to sign on to a UN resolution that explicitly authorized military action.

But on the other side of the world, the real WMD story was unfolding. North Korea expelled international inspectors who had been stationed at Yongbyon to watch over the country's stock of eight thousand fuel rods and its then still-dormant reprocessing plant. The country declared that it was exiting the Nuclear Non-Proliferation Treaty. Soon, spy satellites saw trucks pulling up to the cooling ponds where the fuel rods were being stored, and intelligence analysts quickly concluded that the rods, under surveillance for more than eight years, were about to be moved.

Somewhat incredibly, President Bush was not discussing these activities publicly, nor warning that there was enough weapons-grade material in those rods to manufacture roughly eight nuclear weapons. Had the cooling ponds, the trucks, and the reprocessing center been located north of Baghdad, rather than north of Pyongyang, the president surely would have been on national television warning of the imminent danger to the region and the United States. Instead, the North Korean crisis, if one could call it that, was a distraction, drawing attention away from the number-one priority at the time—disarming Saddam Hussein and ridding his country of WMD that, it famously turned out, he did not possess.

At the *New York Times*, we faced a journalistic conundrum. No one knew at the time, of course, that the Iraqi stockpile was nonexistent. But it seemed abundantly clear that the North Korean decision to move the rods crossed a "red line" that the Clinton administration had set in 1994. At that time, officials asserted that if the rods were moved for reprocessing into weapons fuel, it would be virtually impossible to track them. The Bush administration issued no such warning about losing track of the North's fissile material, because it believed that the North's threat was not credible.

The *Times*' response—after some pushing and pulling between reporters and editors—was to publish a series of front-page stories that suggested the Bush administration was looking for its WMD in all the wrong places. On February 27, 2003—just one day after Secretary of State Colin Powell said there was no evidence of revived nuclear activity at Yongbyon—the paper reported that the North had restarted its five-megawatt reactor at Yongbyon so that it could begin producing more nuclear fuel rods.[2] "The latest move, one American official acknowledged tonight," the paper reported, "will make it harder for the Bush administration to 'take the position that this isn't a crisis.'" The North Korean leadership warned its own citizenry that they could be the next target, after Iraq.

Two days later, just as the administration went before the UN to demand that Saddam Hussein cede power to head off a war, the *Times* returned to the theme of the North Korean nuclear developments. It reported that President Bush was being warned by his own intelligence agencies that the North had restarted its reactor at Yongbyon, a move that would generate more plutonium for nuclear weapons. The North, it appeared, was likewise ready to reactivate its reprocessing facility (also at Yongbyon) to begin extracting plutonium from spent fuel rods. "Once they start reprocessing, it's a bomb a month from now until summer," one official predicted. Clearly, this official was concerned that the administration was not focusing on North Korea.

The administration's response to these stories was to tell *Times* reporters and editors that it was they who were focused on the wrong problem. Condoleezza Rice, then the national security adviser, argued that because Saddam Hussein lived "in a worse neighborhood," his suspected weapons were of far greater concern. He had the ability, she asserted, to destabilize the entire Middle East. North Korea, in contrast, was a bad regime in a good neighborhood, surrounded by strong powers that have a great interest in retaining stability. Yes, North Korea might proceed with an expansion of its nuclear weapons stockpile. But once it had six or eight or even ten weapons, she appeared to be saying, what could it do with them?

The question seemed to answer itself. A nation with one or two weapons cannot risk testing them, much less selling them. A nation with a small surplus in its arsenal can put a few weapons on the market, or at least threaten to do so. Plainly, if Saddam had managed to obtain even one or two weapons, the administration would have raised the alarm that he would soon sell them to al-Qaeda, or seek to use them to dominate the Middle East. But in North Korea's case, such possibilities were rarely uttered in public.

Perhaps the administration's silence was based on a cool-headed assessment of the situation. After all, no two nuclear states are truly alike, in capabilities or intentions. Nonetheless, in the first week of March 2003, just days before the invasion of Iraq, the Pentagon quietly deployed two dozen bombers to Guam, within easy reach of North Korea.[4] But President Bush did not discuss the move publicly; instead, he talked almost exclusively about Iraq, using a prime-time news conference to declare, "I will not leave the American people at the mercy of the Iraqi dictator and his weapons." When he was asked at the same news conference about the evidence that North Korea was racing toward the production of more nuclear fuel, the president said that the problem was a "regional issue."[5]

Such statements raise fundamental questions about the role of reporters, editors, and their newspapers at critical moments in history. Is it possible to conduct sustained coverage of a problem like the North Korea nuclear crisis without appearing to push the country toward a specific response, including military action? Within the parameters of neutral reporting, how far can reporters go in highlighting the huge capability gap between a country the president describes as an "imminent threat" and another whose programs are far more developed but that he does not want to discuss, because his options to stop it are so limited?

Warnings of Tests: A Mix of Intelligence and Politics

In September 2004, two months before the presidential election, a senior administration official ended an interview on another subject at the White House with a revelation: spy satellites had detected a series of actions in North Korea "that we believe would be associated with a test" of a nuclear device. The official made it clear that Washington believed that the activity was related to the forthcoming U.S. presidential election and wanted to send a warning to the North that they were mistaken if they believed they could influence the outcome.

The *Times* was clearly being used, first by the Bush administration, then by the Democratic candidate, John Kerry, who read the resulting article and called the paper to say that the North Korean threat was a reminder of how the Bush administration had failed in its North Korea policy. The official's revelation therefore put the *Times* in a journalistic quandary. What should the newspaper do with news of a potentially important intelligence development that was wrapped in all kinds of political calculation? For years the intelligence community had been watching a test site in North Korea for suspected activity, and at various times it had sent up alarms. So far, all had proved to be false.

The *Times'* solution was to load the article with qualifiers. The top of the story read as follows:

> President Bush and his top advisers have received intelligence reports in recent days describing a confusing series of actions by North Korea that some experts believe could indicate the country is preparing to conduct its first test explosion of a nuclear weapon, according to senior officials with access to the intelligence.
>
> While the indications were viewed as serious enough to warrant a warning to the White House, American intelligence agencies appear divided about the significance of the new North Korean actions, much as they were about the evidence concerning Iraq's alleged weapons stockpiles.
>
> Some analysts in agencies that were the most cautious about the Iraq findings have cautioned that they do not believe the activity detected in North Korea in the past three weeks is necessarily the harbinger of a test. A senior scientist who assesses nuclear intelligence says the new evidence "is not conclusive," but is potentially worrisome.[6]

When Senator Kerry complained the next day that the administration had focused so intensely on Iraq that it had allowed North Korea to speed ahead with developing its arsenal, that charge, too, got front-page play. The paper's critics claimed that it was once again falling for false intelligence.

But what would have been the greater journalistic sin? Would it have been withholding news of warnings the president received about a possible imminent test, whether out of concern for the reliability of American intelligence or out of fear that the intelligence was being twisted for political purposes? Or would it have been publishing the information that had reached the president, with the knowledge that the activity spotted by the satellites could have been less than met the eye, or even a deliberate North Korean deception? It is a difficult choice. In the end, newspapers are in the news business, and if reporters believe that the intelligence community has issued a bona fide warning, that is news. Of course, it must be cast in the right context, with appropriate skepticism, and that was what the *Times* did.

As it happened, the report was not false but merely premature. Two years later, satellites picked up essentially the same pattern of activity. Again, the *Times* reported on these developments in detail. This time, the warnings were correct, as they directly preceded the October 9, 2006, nuclear test—a test that changed the security calculations of Northeast Asia.

North Korea and Iran: Parallel Problems

This choice comes up almost monthly these days with respect to Iran. As with North Korea, the existence of Iran's nuclear program is well known, but its actual workings are little understood. The Iranians demand that the world take them at their word about their current capabilities, yet elements of Iran's program were hidden for eighteen years and experts suspect that facilities may exist that no inspector has ever seen. So far, the most reliable intelligence comes from the International Atomic Energy Agency, whose inspectors have regular, if limited, access to Iran's few declared nuclear sites. But as with North Korea in the 1990s, these inspectors have no access to alternative programs that may be underway in other parts of the country. Mention this in print, however, and a predictable outcry comes back: news organizations are once again unthinkingly leading the country to confrontation.

In short, the moment has come to discuss how proliferation threats should be covered in a post-Iraq world. Reporters must decide whether credible-sounding intelligence findings are news, and determine how to report those findings with appropriate skepticism. Most important, news organizations must consider, in their drive to avoid repeating errors made in the run-up to Iraq, whether they risk creating a whole new class of reportorial mistakes.

Notes

[1] For the best discussion of this period, see Ashton B. Carter and William J. Perry, *Preventive Defense: A New Security Strategy for America* (Washington, DC: Brookings Institution Press, 1999).

[2] David E. Sanger, "Reactor Started in North Korea, U.S. Concludes," *New York Times*, February 27, 2003, A1.

[3] David E. Sanger, "U.S. Sees Quick Start of North Korea Nuclear Site," *New York Times*, March 1, 2003, A1.

[4] David E. Sanger, and Thom Shanker, "U.S. Sending Two Dozen Bombers in Easy Range of North Koreans," *New York Times*, March 5, 2003, A1.

[5] David E. Sanger and Felicity Barringer, "President Readies U.S. for Prospect of Imminent War," *New York Times*, March 7, 2003, A1.

[6] David E. Sanger and William J. Broad, "Fresh Concerns on Atomic Moves by North Korea," *New York Times*, September 12, 2004, A1.

PUBLIC
DIPLOMACY

South Koreans participate in a candlelight vigil in Seoul.
Credit: Reuters/Han Jae-Ho.

PUBLIC DIPLOMACY
AND THE KOREAN PENINSULA

David Straub

I t is a truism among diplomats that even the best public diplomacy cannot effectively promote a policy that a foreign "target audience" believes is not in its interests. But this truism, however correct, does not begin to capture the difficulties of one nation trying to persuade another.

Different peoples frequently regard the same events in very different ways, based on their respective collective memories and sense of national identity. One nation's journalists, sharing the views of their compatriots, often report in a manner that intensifies popular grievances. The media distill events into a simplified dramatic story line that engages their audience's emotions. Citizens become angered by the alleged misdeeds and malign motives of the other country, and they seek out further such media reports, a phenomenon psychologists call confirmation bias. The media eagerly oblige with additional coverage. In such circumstances, attempts at explanation and justification by a foreign state are often regarded cynically, and public diplomacy then can hurt rather than help bilateral ties.

U.S.–South Korean relations provide a valuable case study in the uses and limits of public diplomacy. The reflections in this chapter are drawn from my experiences as a U.S. Foreign Service officer working on Korean affairs from 1999 to 2004 in Seoul and Washington, D.C. They illustrate the complexities and challenges of the political and media environment in which U.S. public diplomacy operates, even when the country in question is a strong ally such as South Korea.

Most South Koreans in today's politically dominant "386 generation" would probably say that America's role in the Kwangju incident of May 1980 convinced them that the United States is not the benevolent protecting power that they had been taught to believe in. They suspect that the United States supported the rise of Maj. Gen. Chun Doo-hwan from late 1979 because the United States felt that another military-backed dictatorship in South Korea—as opposed to a democratic government—would be easier to deal with and would support U.S. interests more fully. The 386ers further believe that when the South Korean military forces supporting Chun engaged in brutal violence against pro-democracy protesters in Kwangju, the United States again chose to back Chun rather than the Korean people.

It does not matter that American officials involved in Korean affairs at the time regarded events and their own actions from a quite different perspective. They felt that the U.S. role in South Korea was primarily to defend it against

North Korea. They were well aware of Chun's ambitions and did not in fact like him, but they were reluctant to intervene in South Korean domestic politics. Such interference, they believed, would be not only inappropriate but also probably ineffective. So troubled were the two then-most-senior U.S. officials in Korea about what they regarded as South Korean misperceptions that, two decades later, after they had retired, each spent years researching and writing memoirs of the events. Ambassador William H. Gleysteen, Jr., wrote *Massive Entanglement, Marginal Influence*, reflecting in the title his view of the U.S. predicament in South Korea.[1] The U.S. Forces in Korea (USFK) commander, General John A. Wickham, wrote *Korea on the Brink: A Memoir of Political Intrigue and Military Crisis*.[2]

By the year 2000, when Ambassador Gleysteen and General Wickham published their memoirs, the South Korean generation that had come of age during that period had long since formed a powerful collective memory of events. Gleysteen's and Wickham's books were translated into Korean, but I have found very few Koreans who have read them.[3] Basically, South Koreans had long felt they already knew what they needed to know, and the memoirs barely made a dent in Korean thinking about the period.

In 2002, when two South Korean schoolgirls were crushed by a USFK vehicle, millions of South Koreans viewed the accident through a prism of attitudes that had been significantly shaped by this preexisting understanding of America's role in their country. For most Americans, the massive protests that followed the accident came out of the blue. The collective American memory holds that the United States saved the ROK in 1950 from a military invasion from the Communist North and subsequently nurtured the South's near-miraculous economic and political development. What, Americans wondered, could possibly explain daily demonstrations that involved tens and even hundreds of thousands of people protesting an unintended traffic accident? Neither official U.S. government pronouncements about U.S.-Korean relations nor the reporting of the American media over the past half century had provided Americans with a basis for comprehending such an outpouring of Korean anger toward the United States. At first, Americans found the South Korean behavior to be simply inexplicable. As the protests continued, however, Americans became resentful about what they regarded as ingratitude from a people they had helped and whom they had considered to be friends and allies.

Of course, South Koreans felt as they did about the 2002 USFK traffic accident for explicable reasons. Unfortunately, these reasons were too complex for most Americans to understand. They involved South Koreans' understanding of their own history—including, but not limited to, America's role in it—and national identity.

For their part, South Koreans failed to understand not only how Americans felt but also why they themselves felt as they did. The South Korean media offered specific reasons to criticize the USFK and the U.S. government's handling of the traffic accident, but those reasons reflected South Korean culture and history. Culture and history, indeed, drove most South Koreans' response to the event, yet like people everywhere, they did not understand even the concept of cultural difference.

When a Korean student who had spent most of his life in the United States shot to death thirty-two people at Virginia Tech in early 2007, almost all South Koreans were immediately deeply concerned. They feared that individual racist Americans would avenge the students' deaths by attacking Koreans living in the United States and that the entire American population would be angry with the Korean people. Even well-educated, cosmopolitan South Koreans worried that the U.S. government would drop the Korea–U.S. Free Trade Agreement (KORUS FTA) and that the U.S. embassy in Seoul might cease to issue visas to Koreans who wished to visit or study in the United States.

Following the tragedy, it took at least a week for South Koreans' fears to abate. Throughout that period, many Americans told the South Korean media that Americans did not feel and would not react in the way that Koreans were concerned they would. U.S. officials offered assurances that the United States had no intention of suspending visa issuances or canceling the KORUS FTA. The South Korean media and most Koreans initially greeted such American assertions with profound skepticism. But after a week had passed and no significant anti-Korean incidents occurred in the United States, South Koreans began to relax. At that point, the South Korean media began to focus approvingly on explanations—put forward both by Americans and by some Korean experts on the United States—that took into account cultural differences between the two countries, particularly with respect to national and ethnic identity.

If you ask South Koreans today about their initial reaction to the 2002 USFK traffic accident, some will concede that it may have been too intense. They will add that, nevertheless, the U.S. government should have responded in a more "responsible" manner. Many South Koreans believe also that U.S. authorities should have engaged in much better public diplomacy. This attitude fits neatly with South Koreans' collective understanding of the United States' role in their country, but it does not explain the events of the period, including U.S. actions. In fact, the South Korean public had been primed for an emotional reaction to the USFK traffic accident by South Korean media reporting, which became increasingly critical of the United States from about 1999 onward.

In the fall of 1999, shortly after I had begun working in Seoul as the head of the political section in the U.S. embassy, the Associated Press began to publish a series of investigative articles about a massacre of South Korean refugees that U.S. military personnel had perpetrated near the village of No Gun Ri in 1950, during the first months of the Korean War.[4] This story was the spark that lit a firestorm of critical South Korean media reporting about the United States. The flames were fanned by the approach of the fiftieth anniversary of the outbreak of the Korean War and by President Kim Dae-jung's unprecedented summit meeting with his North Korean counterpart in June 2000, which led many South Koreans to feel that North Korea was no longer an enemy and that the U.S. military presence was no longer necessary.

In the weeks and months following the Associated Press series, the Korean media reported story after negative story about the United States; the USFK was an especially popular target. Such stories included controversy over the Status of Forces Agreement (SOFA),[5] South Korean soldiers' exposure to Agent Orange during the Vietnam War,[6] an incident at the U.S. Air Force (USAF) practice bombing range near Maehyang-ni,[7] and the dumping by USFK personnel of formaldehyde in the Han River in Seoul.[8] Even a South Korean short-track skater's loss of a medal at the 2002 Winter Olympics in Utah due to an Australian referee's call resulted in sustained South Korean media and public anger at the United States.[9]

If asked, many South Koreans today would say it was President George W. Bush, especially his North Korea policy, that caused them to be critical of the United States in those years. But, in fact, anti-American feelings ran extremely high in South Korea *before* Bush's election as president. U.S.–South Korean tensions were serious in 2000, the last year of the Clinton administration, even as President Clinton was cooperating closely with President Kim Dae-jung on North Korea and attempting to deal responsibly with South Korean grievances about USFK and other political-military issues. Top U.S. embassy and USFK officials devoted themselves to dealing with the South Korean media's negative reporting about the United States. In some cases, the Korean media grossly exaggerated stories, such as the formaldehyde incident noted earlier.[10] In other cases, such as the USAF training accident,[11] the media almost entirely invented stories. The South Korean media routinely portrayed USFK personnel as being on a criminal rampage against the Korean people, even though USFK statistics I saw in the U.S. embassy at the time showed a long-term downward trend in the number of serious crimes committed by USFK personnel against South Koreans. The South Korean media uncritically reported statements by South Korean nongovernmental organizations (NGOs)—some of which clearly had an anti-USFK agenda—that portrayed minor traffic and parking violations by USFK personnel as serious crimes.

Deeply concerned about this phenomenon, I had long talks with the U.S. embassy's press spokesman. He explained to me that media often have a story line that reflects editors' and reporters' views, or that appeals to their readers, or both. By the year 2000, the story line of South Korean reporters, many of whom belonged to the 386 generation, boiled down to a single theme—the U.S. government, especially the USFK, disrespected the Korean people to the extent of not caring about their safety or even their lives. The negative articles were legion: Americans had killed innocent Korean refugees at No Gun Ri, USFK mortuary workers were pouring poison into the Han River, the USAF was dropping bombs on a Korean village for target practice. The SOFA, by unanimous opinion, was held to be grossly unfair to South Korea. The South

Korean media reporting quickly became a vicious cycle. Items that fit into the "ugly American" story line were covered; those that did not were not highlighted. As popular anger grew, so did the appetite for even more negative stories about the United States.

USFK and U.S. embassy leaders devoted an enormous amount of time and attention to trying to deal with these incidents and reports. They met with and briefed Korean reporters, talked and negotiated with South Korean officials, strengthened USFK procedures, issued statements of explanation and regret, and reported back to Washington. South Koreans who supported a close relationship with the United States would often privately upbraid U.S. officials in Seoul for not engaging in more active public diplomacy. What they did not grasp was that the South Korean media's story line had become so tendentious that almost all Koreans greeted U.S. statements and explanations with disbelief and anger. The South Korean media reported, and the public agreed, that America had no sense of shame. The United States, they felt, was trying to defend the indefensible, and any explanation to the contrary just made the situation worse.

Very few South Koreans, even those who were pro-American or conservative, spoke out against the dominant critical attitude toward the United States during that period. National feeling was running so strong that South Koreans who were concerned about relations with the United States or who disagreed with media portrayals were apparently afraid to publicize their opinions. It took several years before the climate began to change and a tipping point was reached.

Most South Koreans worry about a perceived asymmetry in the power relationship between their country and the United States. What most South Koreans and Americans do not realize, however, is that, with respect to media reporting on the bilateral relationship, a significant asymmetry exists *in South Korea's favor*. The Korean media report far more extensively on U.S.–South Korean relations than do the U.S. media. Naturally, they report from a South Korean perspective. Overall, the result is that South Korea frames issues and sets the agenda for the relationship to a significant degree, despite the United States' being the more powerful player.

The USAF training incident is a particularly instructive example. In May 2000, the USAF in South Korea had a single training range for target practice, located near the village of Maehyang-ni, on the Yellow Sea coast southwest of Seoul. During this period, a USAF plane developed mechanical difficulties. Following standard procedures, the pilot dropped the bombs he was carrying onto the range and returned safely to base. In the village, the longtime leader of a movement to end USAF training at the range immediately informed the South Korean media that there had been a major incident. He also noted, among other things, that old people had injured themselves fleeing in panic, and that the walls of houses had been cracked by the explosions. The South Korean media reported the charges uncritically and in great detail. Editorials expressed outrage for days, demanding an apology and an investigation.

In response, USFK and the Korean defense ministry conducted a joint investigation. They spent nearly a week at the site, inspecting houses, taking photographs, and conducting interviews. Their joint conclusion was that it was impossible for the incident to have caused the alleged damage. However, when the U.S. major general heading the American team proposed to put that finding in the official report, as he told me at the time, his South Korean counterpart pleaded with him at least to note, falsely, that there had been some damage. Otherwise, he explained, the Korean media and public reaction would be extremely negative. The public believed that the incident had caused major problems and would not accept anything to the contrary. The U.S. general refused to sign his name to a false report, and the report was issued stating that no damage had occurred. The South Korean media indeed responded with outrage, charging in numerous editorials that the United States did not understand that the problem was not just the one incident but rather the long history of harm that the USAF training range had caused to the people of the village.

I personally was deeply disturbed about South Korean media reports that suggested USFK personnel were on a criminal rampage. As an American official, I was concerned both about the safety of the Korean people and about the damage to U.S.-Korean relations. I wanted to know if the crime situation was as serious as it was reported to be by the Korean media. If it was, I felt strongly that action should be taken. As mentioned earlier, USFK statistics showed that serious crime by USFK personnel was significantly down. But was the current level acceptable? I asked myself: How does the USFK crime rate compare, for example, to that of the South Korean military? I telephoned the defense ministry, explained the situation, and asked where I could find such statistics. (Both the U.S. and the South Korean governments publish all USFK crime statistics.) The South Korean official hesitated, but finally said he doubted such statistics would be of much use since South Korean military personnel stayed on their bases most of the time. I persisted, saying that, nevertheless, it would help me to have at least a benchmark so I could put the data into perspective. After another pause, he said, "I'm sorry. I can't give you the crime statistics on ROK military personnel. They're classified 'confidential.'"

President George W. Bush's unpopularity among South Koreans was another factor that worsened South Korean attitudes toward the United States after 2001. This was especially true after President Kim Dae-jung met with him at the White House in March 2001 to discuss—unsuccessfully—North Korea policy. Furthermore, like many other people, South Koreans opposed President Bush's invasion of Iraq.

Ironically, in the years since the U.S. invasion of Iraq, South Koreans' feelings toward the United States have improved significantly, while their attitude toward North Korea has taken an almost equally sharp downturn.[12] U.S. public diplomacy professionals, both in Seoul and Washington, have certainly worked hard in recent years to nurture the U.S.-ROK relationship, but their efforts have had little influence. Instead, a number of other factors have played a part, including the following:

- The 2002 candlelight demonstrations against the accidental USFK killing of the two schoolgirls provided a public catharsis, as the South Korean public felt it had made its point about perceived U.S. insensitivity.
- After his election as president in 2002, Roh Moo-hyun expressed his desire to work with the United States, an attitude that mitigated the South Korean media's negativity.
- South Koreans later renounced President Roh, primarily over domestic policy and character issues, taking the focus off the United States.
- Popular doubts about the South Korean government's North Korea policy grew after Pyongyang repeatedly failed to demonstrate sincerity, making some South Koreans feel that perhaps President Bush's hard-line approach to North Korea was not so objectionable.

During the period 1999–2002, the American media covered most of the major issues in U.S.–South Korean relations. The U.S. media were unable, however, to present a complete picture to readers and viewers, due largely to the complexity of the situation and the inherent limitations of reporting on foreign affairs for a general American audience. This was particularly true of U.S. reporting on South Korea's handling of the Iraq issue. When the U.S. government, eager to demonstrate that it had the backing of the international community for its occupation of Iraq, asked South Korea to send troops to the country, President Roh agonized over the decision.[13] His political base strongly opposed such a dispatch, and he personally believed that the American invasion and occupation of Iraq was unwarranted.

Ultimately, however, President Roh personally appealed to the National Assembly to approve the dispatch of South Korean troops. He argued publicly that while the American invasion and occupation of Iraq could not be morally justified, the ROK had to send troops there for the sake of its alliance with the United States. In context, what he meant—a point perfectly clear to South Koreans—was that he feared the United States might be more inclined to take unilateral action against North Korea for its nuclear program if the ROK did not support the U.S. invasion.

At the time, the U.S. media barely touched upon this fact. Indeed, most of them simply repeated the Bush administration's statements about how South Korea was the third-largest contributor of troops to Iraq, after the United States and the United Kingdom, and how this deployment reflected the vitality of the U.S.-ROK alliance and widespread international support for U.S. policy in Iraq. Externally, President Roh and other South Korean officials characterized their actions similarly, primarily because Roh wished to protect himself from criticism from South Korean conservatives. Also left largely unreported was the fact that, like Japan, South Korea sent troops only on the condition that they would be deployed to one of the safest places in Iraq—that is, to an area where their presence did not contribute directly to improving the security situation.

One might say, therefore, that the ROK deployment to Iraq was bad on four points. First, South Koreans regarded the American invasion and occupation of Iraq as immoral. Second, they felt forced to deploy their troops to Iraq to gain leverage over U.S. policy on North Korea. Third, both the South Korean and the American governments used the situation to mislead their respective peoples about the state of U.S.-ROK relations. Finally, the South Korean deployment did not help to provide security for the people of Iraq.

The American media did, however, have a significant impact on U.S. policy toward South Korea during President Chun Doo-hwan's rule from 1980 to 1988. President Reagan directed most of his attention at that time toward countering the Soviet Union; he believed that the human rights abuses of right-wing authoritarian governments were a lesser, and less immediate, concern. When such governments were friends or allies of the United States, as was Chun's South Korea, Reagan's policy was to use so-called quiet diplomacy to encourage them to engage in more democratic practices.

Though Reagan's critics would assert otherwise, quiet diplomacy was not just a catchphrase. Throughout Reagan's two terms in office, the U.S. government pressed Chun to liberalize, and it insisted especially that he keep his promise to step down after a single term. Nevertheless, U.S. criticism of the South Korean human rights situation was considerably less forceful under Reagan than it had been under President Jimmy Carter.

The American media took a more vocal stance against Chun's suppression of democracy and human rights than did the Reagan administration, a stance that kept the issue very much alive in Washington policy councils and encouraged Chun's South Korean opponents. Working on the Korea Desk at the State Department from 1984 to 1986, I spent most mornings drafting and clearing press guidance on the latest reports of Chun's imprisonment and torture of South Korean politicians and human rights activists. The State Department's press spokesperson used these notes to prepare for the daily noon press briefing. Certainly, South Koreans themselves played the decisive role in bringing about their country's democratization in 1987. Yet the American media played a significant supporting role, by forcing the State Department to respond to reports of South Korean government abuses of its own people, and by publicizing those reports in the United States. Partly as a result, the Reagan administration responded in 1987 to massive South Korean popular protests against Chun by pressing him not to crack down but to liberalize.

Among the many hindrances to effective U.S. public diplomacy is the fact that most embassy officials do not speak the local language beyond a rudimentary level; their understanding of the history and culture of the host country is also limited. U.S. embassy officials usually work only about a thousand days in any given country, hardly long enough to even begin to understand it well. Occasionally, U.S. officials serve a second or even a third tour in a country, but the number of officials at an embassy with deep experience in that country is usually small. A second and even greater impediment to effective public diplomacy—not to mention foreign policy in general—stems from our cultural and nationalistic biases, of which we are often only dimly aware. The people of every country have their own lens through which they look at the world, and that lens can severely distort analysis of events and produce responses that are emotional and misdirected.

In the 1980s and early 1990s, I served for six years at the U.S. embassy in Tokyo. During this period, the U.S. government and the U.S. media were fixated on what appeared to be Japan's trajectory to surpass the United States as the world's largest economy. Americans generally believed one of two theories on this subject. The decidedly minority view, put forward by Harvard professor Ezra Vogel in his book *Japan as Number One*, held that the Japanese system was superior in important respects.[14] The majority view in the United States, however, was that Japan was surging ahead due to unfair, mercantilist trading practices.[15] Most Americans felt great anger toward Japan, and the Japanese, in turn, were offended by the American reaction. Official relations were also poisoned by these perceptions. Soon after the Japanese economic bubble burst in the early 1990s, American concern about the Japanese economic "threat" rapidly faded. It is clear now that both American arguments—that Japan had a better system and that it was cheating—were largely beside the point. Japan had, in fact, experienced an enormous bubble, based on real estate and stock market speculation, not unlike the current crisis in the United States. In hindsight, it is amazing that such a huge pyramid scheme was not readily apparent to all, Americans and Japanese alike. That it was not, I believe, can be attributed in part to the national "lenses" and the nationalistic reactions in both countries.

Even more disturbing is that Americans, including those in the government and the media, scarcely reflected on the lessons of the U.S.-Japanese "trade war." We should have learned that nationalistic agendas can make us extremely emotional and prevent society as a whole from coming to reasonable, balanced conclusions. Our experiences in both Japan and South Korea should have taught us to be more modest, not only about our ability to understand foreign countries but also about our capacity to influence them. These are not just theoretical issues. For example, if we failed to grasp something as basic as a speculative bubble in an open, democratic U.S. ally like Japan, how could we imagine we could reshape other, more traditional countries, such as Afghanistan and Iraq?

Americans are not alone in having difficulty understanding other countries and cultures. South Koreans, as I noted, have reacted in a similarly nationalistic and culturally blinkered way toward the United States, especially during the period 1999–2002. However, the extent of American power makes American failings more readily apparent, at least to outside observers, and sometimes also more damaging.

None of the foregoing observations is meant to suggest that public diplomacy is not important. On the contrary, it is an essential element of foreign and security policies, and should be funded accordingly. But the reflections in this chapter suggest that public diplomacy cannot be effective unless it is in support of a reasonable foreign policy. With a sound foreign policy to promote, public diplomacy can be very effective. In the case of an unsound foreign policy, however, public diplomacy will likely be feckless. In the end, to be sound, a foreign policy—and not just the public diplomacy that serves it—must recognize and take into account the target country's political and cultural perspectives.

Notes

[1] William H. Gleysteen, Jr., *Massive Entanglement, Marginal Influence: Carter and Korea in Crisis* (Washington, DC: Brookings Institution Press, 2000).

[2] John A. Wickham and Richard Holbrooke, *Korea on the Brink: A Memoir of Political Intrigue and Military Crisis* (Dulles, VA: Brassey's Inc., 2000).

[3] In an unpublished interview conducted in Seoul on February 10, 2006, by Daniel C. Sneider, associate director for research of Stanford University's Shorenstein Asia-Pacific Research Center, former president Kim Dae-jung said he had not read Gleysteen's memoirs. This is a remarkable acknowledgement coming from a person who was a key figure in the events discussed in Gleysteen's book and who is known to be a voracious reader.

[4] See Sang-Hun Choe and Charles J. Hanley, "Ex-GIs Tell AP of Korea Killings," Associated Press, September 30, 1999, http://www.washingtonpost.com/wp-srv/aponline/19990930/aponline065913_000.htm. See also the book on the same subject later written by the coauthors of the AP series: Charles J. Hanley, Sang-hun Choe, and Martha Mendoza, *The Bridge at No Gun Ri: A Hidden Nightmare from the Korean War* (New York: Henry Holt, 2001).

[5] Shin Yong-bae, "Korea, U.S. to Resume SOFA Revision Talks," *Korea Herald*, October 11, 1999.

[6] Lee Sung-yul, "Defense Minister Cho Calls for Probe into Spray of Toxic Defoliants in DMZ," *Korea Herald*, November 17, 1999.

[7] Kang Seok-jae, "7 Koreans Injured as U.S. Fighter Makes Emergency Bomb Drop," *Korea Herald*, May 12, 2000.

[8] Kang Seok-jae, "USFK Secretly Dumped Toxic Chemicals into Han River, Civic Group Claims," *Korea Herald*, July 14, 2000.

[9] *Korea Times*, "Controversial Ruling Costs Korea Gold," February 22, 2002.

[10] Chang Jae-soon, "Civic Groups Demand USFK Chief's Resignation over Dumping Incident," *Korea Herald*, July 15, 2000.

[11] Editorial, *Korea Herald*, "Plight of Maehyang-ni Residents," May 13, 2000.

[12] See, for example, the Pew Global Attitudes Project, "Global Unease with Major World Powers," June 27, 2007, http://pewglobal.org/reports/display.

php?ReportID=256. For Asian opinion polls since 2004, see the Maureen and Mike Mansfield Foundation, "The Mansfield Asian Opinion Poll Database," http://www.mansfieldfdn.org/polls/polls_listing.htm.

[13] *Korea Times*, "Roh Appeals to Nation to Back Troop Dispatch," April 3, 2003. In a speech to the National Assembly the previous day, President Roh reportedly said, "I decided on the dispatch in anguish because the fate of the country and the people would depend on my decision."

[14] Ezra Vogel, *Japan as Number One: Lessons for America* (Rutland, VT: Tuttle, 1980).

[15] See especially Karel van Wolferen, *The Enigma of Japanese Power: People and Politics in a Stateless Nation* (New York: Knopf, 1989).

THE MEDIA'S ROLE IN U.S. POLICY
TOWARD THE KOREAS

Chris Nelson

In late 2006, in the weeks immediately after the November election's Republican sweeps, something very interesting began to happen to the Bush administration's North Korea policy. Suddenly, it became the nearly exclusive property of President Bush himself. The policy filtered back and forth between the Oval Office and Secretary of State Condoleezza Rice, while Chris Hill, the assistant secretary for East Asia and the Pacific, both initiated and implemented the policies that gave rise to most of the events that have happened since.

President Bush's increased involvement during this period seems to have limited the role that the Korea Desk at the State Department—the "traditional" policymaking apparatus for the Koreas—was able to play in the region. To explain the failed Bush policy toward North Korea, particularly during the tenure of Secretary of Defense Donald Rumsfeld, many White House insiders have argued that Rice, then national security advisor, and Mike Green, then senior director for Asia, were doomed from the start. Whatever intelligent thing they wanted to do was nearly automatically checked—even checkmated—by the alliance between Rumsfeld and Vice President Dick Cheney. Once Rumsfeld was removed from the equation, along with United Nations ambassador John Bolton and then National Security Council official Robert Joseph (who was later State Department deputy assistant secretary), the Bush-Rice-Hill triple wing actually had room to run in an open field.

It is a truism that people are policy and that the policymaking process becomes highly personalized at the top levels. Such personalization can help to get things done, but it can also hamper both open media and the careful use of closed intelligence assessments. Simply put, if the person running the show permits no one to meaningfully cover his or her activities, we can only hope that the boss has good instincts and, more important, good luck.

Taking into account the above-mentioned shifts in policymaking responsibility between 2002 and late 2006, it is fair to say that print media and academic journals played a leading role in helping shape the opposition to what became a failed Bush policy—its failure being that it did not stop North Korea from developing and testing a nuclear weapon. After that time, however, and after Rice gave Ambassador Hill permission to negotiate directly with North Korea, the press largely lagged behind events. From that point on, the media's coverage was reactive rather than formative, for the obvious reason that Hill and his counterparts had much more control of the events. In fact, as I will discuss later in this chapter, Hill manipulated the media very cleverly. He marshaled the press to change not only the prior administration's claims but also the actual negotiating position on the "secret" highly enriched uranium program. In 2002 the Bush administration had cited the existence of this program as the reason—or excuse—for stopping all negotiations with Pyongyang. More generally, the North Korea experience (like that of Iraq) epitomizes the risks journalists face in trying to balance their access to policymakers with accurate reporting on what those policymakers are saying. For reporting to be "accurate," journalists must be able to provide a level of informed interpretation—something more than a literal transcription of official remarks; but offering such a perspective is often easier said than done. Indeed, any study of the Bush administration's relationship with the media will note the former's use of calculated intimidation and open punishment to inspire fear in the latter. These methods were apparent, even before 9/11, in the administration's treatment of reporters and commentators. Though seemingly mild, punishment was characterized by loss of access. Gone were the little privileges that can help to distinguish a journalist's work and also make his or her life easier: being invited to small private meetings, getting calls and e-mails returned, being told, for example, "But seriously, on background you can say . . ." The Bush people did not invent this game—the Obama administration will no doubt use it also—but they played it very, very well.

Reporters and editors for the *Washington Post* and the *New York Times*, in effect the U.S. "papers of record" for most of the world, must try to define "accurate reporting" as something beyond what they are being told by senior administration foreign policy and intelligence officials. The fact that statements are made may be literally "true." But in both Iraq and North Korea, the media have often not reported on the reliability of these official statements using time-tested (if unclassified) public resources easily available on the Internet, not to mention the good old-fashioned telephone. Simply put, many critics have argued that the *New York Times*, the *Washington Post*, and other major newspapers failed—despite what may have been the best intentions—to provide a fully balanced perspective on official U.S government statements about North Korea. Had these reporters dug deeper and scrutinized the statements more carefully, they would have immediately discovered widespread skepticism among Korea- and nonproliferation-watchers. Indeed, many of these specialists readily offered (to other media, such as blogs and specialty newsletters) very specific, fact-based assessments that discounted the likelihood of a pending North Korean nuclear test.

Critics have also noted that much of the coverage during 2002–2006 did not place the official statements into a larger context. How, for example, might they fit into the Bush administration's major policy goals, such as seeking greater unity among the participants of the Six-Party Talks in presenting a harder line to North Korea? Or, how would the statements naturally reinforce U.S. and Japanese public support for national missile defense? In other words, concerned critics and readers throughout the foreign policy and nonproliferation communities have concluded that the net effect of much recent U.S. North Korea coverage was not just misleading but also false, and thus a failure on the part of both the reporters and their editors. But at the time, to the average reader, it seemed that the major newspapers were accurately reporting on U.S. intelligence.

Some papers and news organizations did better than others.[1] The main point here, however, is that journalism is a hard job at the best of times, complicated by the need to keep up with multiple, often conflicting, and sometimes competing sources, in and out of government, in several directly involved nations. Journalists must use their best professional judgment, based on their own experience and that of people they trust, in order to make sense of the information at their disposal

In this context, it is worth considering the relationship between then assistant secretary of state Chris Hill and the news media. Hill was no shrinking violet; he appeared to enjoy what passes for cut and thrust in the media today. Moreover, he absolutely understood how to "use" the press to send messages to North Korea, South Korea, China, and Japan. Beginning in early 2007, Hill began to carefully backpedal on the Bush administration's claims of 2002 and 2003 that North Korea was conducting a secret highly enriched uranium (HEU) program that contravened the 1994 Agreed Framework. For years, White House press briefings and congressional testimony gave the distinct impression not only that the Bush administration had uncovered yet another thing the Clinton administration had missed, but also that this secret HEU program was possibly already in production. We now know that both implications were patently false, thanks mainly to Hill's careful statements, but also, notably, because Barbara Slavin wrote a number of stories for *USA Today* that debunked such claims.

Once Hill secured the February 13, 2005, agreement, with its phased requirements, including a full "declaration" by Pyongyang of its entire nuclear program—past, present, and future—it is easy to see why he had already moved, with the cooperation of U.S. intelligence, to retrench, and to redefine, what Washington really thought about North Korea's HEU efforts. Hill highlighted the distinction between an *acquisition* program and an up-and-running *production* program, for which there was not a shred of reliable evidence. Using the press to drive home this distinction, Hill cleverly did an end run around his critics (both those that remained in the administration and those exiled from it) while simultaneously lowering the bar Pyongyang had to jump over to satisfy the HEU portion of the required declaration.

Another administration claim, which seemed to block progress for more than a year—and the sudden revision of which, ironically, blocked it for several months more—was the still complicated, still not fully explained story of the $25 million in North Korean funds that the U.S. froze at Banco Delta Asia (BDA) in Macao. Thanks to months of hard digging by the McClatchy newspapers, especially State Department reporter Warren Strobel, the sequence of events gradually became clearer. The print press, on both sides of the Pacific, played a larger than usual role in shaping the BDA "issue" and in following its apparently successful, if still contradictory, conclusion. BDA will provide a useful case study, if and when the facts all come to light, of the interaction between the media and policymakers, pro and con. In this instance, the McClatchy stories helped Chris Hill on some occasions and harmed U.S. credibility on others.

U.S. policy toward South Korea is, of course, also a critical factor in assessing how to deal with North Korea. The strategic military alliance between the United States and South Korea, and direct consultations on the Six-Party Talks process are obvious points of departure, but we tend to rush right past the economic component of the U.S.-ROK alliance. I would argue that, to an extent that may yet prove definitive, the success or failure of the bilateral economic relationship between the United States and South Korea is joined at the political hip to the nuclear talks.

A second arena that merits careful examination is the "public diplomacy" of the Korea-U.S. Free Trade Agreement (KORUS FTA). There have been a handful of occasionally useful situation reports ("sitreps") on this agreement in the *Times*, the *Financial Times*, and the specialist business newsletter world. However, if you had to rely on either public diplomacy or systematic media coverage to track KORUS through to its current status, you would be out of luck.

KORUS was officially signed on June 30, 2007. It was grandfathered into permanent "fast track" coverage at literally the last minute, even though Trade Promotion Authority (TPA) has now formally expired and may not be renewed. Thus, the deal cannot be officially renegotiated without exposing it to the risk of being amended to death on Capitol Hill.

The next formal step will be for some administration to devise implementing legislation for Congress to approve. Note the qualifier "some"—one of the quirks of U.S. trade law is that once it is signed, you can hold off on implementing an FTA for fifty years, if you think you will need that amount of time to build support to get it approved. Once you do submit the legislation, however, Congress must, under TPA, return an up-or-down, yes-or-no response within ninety legislative days.

The role of public diplomacy and the media can obviously be critical to the approval process of an FTA, and in the case of KORUS, the future does not look promising. Up until midnight on June 30, 2007, the Korean government had understandably focused on striking the delicate balance of designing an FTA that gave enough to Korea so that its legislature would approve the deal, and gave just enough to the United States to win in Congress. The Office of the United States Trade Representative (USTR) had to play the same balancing game, and the immediate prognosis, on both sides of the Pacific, is not so good. Key players in the House Democratic leadership have been arguing some unique interpretations of the trade policy process, including that South Korea must accept binding amendments to KORUS that were not negotiated, and that South Korea's legislature must approve a revised KORUS, before Congress will deign to act at all.

Whether there is an acceptable solution to the KORUS conundrum will depend to a large degree on public diplomacy by and on behalf of the business interests that would benefit from KORUS. That is only now beginning, primarily at the USTR's instigation. There is some concern that it may already be too late because the opposition may already have created an irradicable impression of inequality and negotiating failure.

Since negotiations began, U.S. auto interests in particular have tried to use KORUS to renegotiate the terms by which Korean auto manufacturers were cleared to set up shop in the United States, without any reciprocal moves to alleviate often draconian South Korean barriers to U.S. imports of both cars and parts. While the call for reciprocity is certainly apt, U.S. leverage is nonexistent, given the fait accompli of the Korean plants in the United States. In any event, despite the cries of anguish from Auto Caucus and labor members of Congress, KORUS addresses many, if not most, of the tariff barriers and nontariff barriers at issue between the United States and South Korea. The bottom line, however, is that *if* the administration and the business community ever get their acts together and a coherent lobbying campaign can be mounted on behalf of KORUS, the media will play an important role, both in describing the arguments and driving the internal debate.

The Nelson Report Survey

In preparing this chapter, I conducted an informal survey of *The Nelson Report*[2] sources. My colleagues and I asked these individuals what they thought of the current U.S. policies toward South Korea, and received responses from approximately two dozen men and women who specialize in Korea and related subjects for the departments of State and Defense, on Capitol Hill, and in various trade-related agencies and think tanks. A few fellow journalists also took part. In addition, we heard from former high-ranking officials of various agencies who continue to focus their time and energy on Korea and nuclear nonproliferation.

Above all, we wanted to hear, in their own words, these players' thoughts about the competing news media of the United States, the Koreas, and Japan. We asked five basic, if somewhat extended, questions:

1. What U.S. media sources do you use to learn about the Koreas? Which are the most consistently useful? Do any especially useful examples come to mind that have influenced your decision-making?
2. If you had to rely only on U.S. media sources, would you have sufficient information to do your job? If you do not find the information sufficient, how do you supplement it? Or, do the U.S. media supplement the Korea-based sources?

3. What Korean sources or resources do you use to do your job? Which are the most consistently reliable? In your experience, do these sources accurately convey Korean government positions? Do they accurately convey U.S. government positions?
4. Do you utilize a Korea media listserv, or do you do your own searches? Which listserv do you use and/or which searches do you perform? How often do you access the listserv or do the searches?
5. Does media coverage about the Koreas display a useful balance of political, diplomatic, and nonproliferation topics, or is the focus too much on just one issue?

With respect to the first question, on the effectiveness and reliability of U.S. media sources, the responses of the more than twenty participants were mixed. Most agreed that sometimes the media were more reliable than one might think. However, one well-known U.S. expert (who is himself frequently called for comment) remarked despairingly, "If I had to rely on U.S. media to follow North Korea or inter-Korean relations, I would jump out of a window!"

A former State Department official added to this critique. "U.S. media report rather poorly on the Korean Peninsula," he observed, "because they report less on 'Korea' per se than on U.S.-Korea relations, on the DPRK nuclear/missile issue, and on related intelligence matters. They tend, accordingly, to rely heavily on U.S. official sources for the basic story, and to flesh that out with brief quotes [or] sound bites from U.S. academic and think tank specialists. Few U.S. media seem to weave into their stories information from the ROK media, ROK official sources, or ROK academic and think tank experts."

I quote this extended comment for two reasons. First, it echoes my earlier remarks about the *New York Times'* recent coverage of Korea. Second, it explains precisely why *The Nelson Report* survey focused so heavily on soliciting U.S. comments about Korean media. The fact is, U.S. policymakers and commentators nearly all rely primarily on their own or others' interpretations of Korean media, rather than on original work by the U.S. media. Unfortunately, very few in the U.S. news media pay similar attention to Korean sources.

To be sure, there are reporters who consider the bigger picture, examining both Korean and American perspectives on a given issue, and a handful of journalists received consistent praise from our survey respondents. According to one State Department source, along with several think tank members and former officials, among all U.S. reporters, the best are Barbara Demick of the *Los Angeles Times* and Barbara Slavin, formerly at *USA Today* and now at the *Washington Times*. (Also singled out were the *New York Times* correspondents in Beijing, especially Joe Kahn for his perspectives on Chinese reactions to U.S. policy and to North Korea; Howard W. French and Norimitsu Onishi, also of the *New York Times*; and McClatchy Newspapers' Warren Strobel).

More generally, a majority of respondents said they regularly check the Reuters wire service and the BBC World Service on the Internet, citing them as reliable providers of useful reporting and insight. Although these are not U.S. media per se, they are fully available and utilized by staff and advisers to U.S. policymakers.

Only on trade matters did U.S. players (and other journalists) feel they had access to consistently useful, U.S.-generated coverage about Korea via the *Washington Trade Daily* and the online *Inside U.S. Trade*. The occasional (but thorough) business page coverage of the *Washington Post* and *New York Times* was also cited. With KORUS negotiations now growing more tightly focused and politically "interesting," trade coverage is likely to appear with greater regularity, especially in the *Wall Street Journal*. U.S. policy analysts and decision makers also always mention the London *Financial Times* (FT), since its Tokyo and Beijing bureaus regularly supplement its sophisticated economic and political coverage of U.S. policy. Survey respondents also identified the work of the *International Herald Tribune*'s Choe Sang-hun. As Winston Churchill once quipped, America and Britain are one people divided by a common language. In fact, the acceptance of the FT by both Washington and Wall Street virtually eliminates international boundaries. Indeed, the FT boasts a larger circulation in the United States than in the United Kingdom.

On specific stories related to the Department of Defense (DOD), especially the ongoing and controversial discussion of troop redeployment, all survey respondents identified *Defense News* as reliable, timely, and "invaluable." *The Nelson Report* itself, which seeks to bridge the editorial divide between defense, economic, political, analytic, and commentary reporting, also received praise for its coverage of key issues in these areas.

With respect to question 2, about whether U.S. media provided sufficient information for respondents to do their jobs, and whether U.S. media relied on Korean sources, the answer to the latter was clear—as noted earlier, very few U.S. media avail themselves of Korean resources. As for the former question, a typical assessment came from a former journalist who is now an academic and a commentator:

> I do *not* rely on U.S. media to follow developments in North and South Korea. The U.S. media are adequate for coverage of U.S. policy toward the Koreas, but almost useless when it comes to coverage of the Peninsula itself. American coverage of Korea is skewed way too much toward one subject—the North Korean nuclear problem. . . . Mostly I rely on the Korean media, supplemented by the Japanese media and some online resources. I read the major Korean newspapers online, along with the Yonhap News Agency. I get the daily press summaries of the Japanese media prepared by the U.S. Embassy in Tokyo [other respondents noted receipt of the same service from the U.S. Embassy in Seoul]. I also regularly read the output of North Korea's KCNA [Korean Central News Agency], and of Xinhua, the official Chinese news agency.

Several specific views on the Korean media are worth noting at length, because U.S. experts and a handful of journalists rely so fundamentally on the Korean (as well as Japanese and Chinese) media for story ideas, gossip, perspective, and even the occasional "scoop." As a senior Capitol Hill adviser explained, "I don't use any media sources to learn about Korea in depth; rather, they help me highlight for my boss what *are* the issues, what's big today or might be coming up soon?" This staffer added that "my main challenge is getting perspective on the views and news; therefore I need sophisticated information collection."

Here is how a State Department official described the daily routine of sourcing information about the Koreas:

> The reality is that there is little useful in the U.S. media for a line government person [a government employee working at the nonsenior political appointee level], who is by definition ahead of the regular "news." Therefore, in terms of media, I really rely on the Korean media to get a sense of how issues are being dissected politically. I receive my Korean media digests from three principal sources: the U.S. Embassy daily translations emailed, the former FBIS [Foreign Broadcast Information Service], now called OSC [Open Source Center], and then direct from Korean English-language websites. I am also trying to follow Korean blogs. Overall? The information is never that deep or complex from the standpoint of an inside player, but it's useful in outlining what's on the public's mind.

We did not ask a specific question about U.S. think tanks, but many respondents made a point of praising the Korea-focused programs of the Center for Strategic and International Studies (CSIS), including the center's many publications on various Korea-related topics. Several respondents cited the programs and publications of the Washington, D.C.–based Korea Economic Institute (KEI), which is now very focused on KORUS.

Question 3, about reliable Korean sources and their accuracy in covering the Korean and U.S. governments, received perhaps the most mixed responses. There was, however, unanimous consensus that Yonhap News Agency's daily and weekly coverage is valuable and accurate, especially in presenting South Korean public and government views. Survey respondents also felt that Yonhap was reliable in presenting Korean attitudes about U.S. government policies.

Overall, survey respondents did not identify a single Korean news organization, outlet, or source as consistently and accurately reporting on U.S. government policy. One senior State Department former official summed up a favorable if muted response: "Yonhap News Service does a fine job of reporting all significant developments. *Chosun Ilbo, Joongang Ilbo, Hankook Ilbo,* the *Korea Times* in English, *Donga Ilbo,* and *Hankyoreh* all contain useful information and insights from time to time. But stories in each of these publications needs to be understood in terms of the political orientation of the editorial board of each publication."

In terms of Korean media accuracy regarding the statements of policies of South Korea's administration, the consensus, to quote another U.S. government official, was that "they do so selectively, sometimes out of context, or with a slant that supports a particular attitude toward the government. One would not look to any of the ROK media for a reliable expression of [the administration's] views. The same is even more the case with respect to conveying U.S. government positions, where selective quotation, often with some distortion or misunderstanding, is [frequently] found."

Several respondents noted the deep policy disconnect between the South Korea's pro–North Korea Uri government and the Bush administration on how to deal with, or even think about, the Kim Jong-il regime in the North. This disconnect has led to pronouncements, especially by the Unification Ministry (which handles relations with the North) and by the Blue House, that must be carefully parsed to detect the difference between what these officials wish were the case and what actual U.S. attitudes and policies might be. Such dissection has proved equally necessary with Unification Ministry and Blue House assessments of North Korean actions.

On the use of Korean or Korea-related listservs—the subject of question 4—we were not surprised to discover that survey respondents, whether reporters, analysts, decision makers, or commentators, frequently and often heavily use a variety of government, commercial, and purely labor-of-love listservs. We define a *listserv* as an electronically gathered and disseminated listing of the latest or currently available news stories, magazine articles, think tank pieces, TV and radio reporting, and even book reviews; in short, we consider a listserv to be any organized list of things to read and think about. Because of the foreign policy, defense, and nonproliferation issues at the heart of Korea today, the listserv universe is extraordinarily rich.

The two principal U.S. government listservs are FBIS/OSC and the Defense Department's "Early Bird." The latter is a daily compilation of the latest press, audio transcripts, and magazine stories that the listserv's DOD-based compilers believe that analysts and policymakers in the defense community may find useful. Not all U.S. players have the time or energy to deal with their own listserv, and for these individuals there is the U.S. government–supplied Foreign Broadcast Information Service, formerly known as FBIS and now called the Open Source Center, or OSC, for reasons that are not entirely clear. Nearly every one of our government respondents said they regularly check both the DOD's Early Bird and the OSC.

One DOD analyst remarked, "I do try to read the OSC take most days, which draws pretty extensively on the Korean press, so you get far more in-depth coverage of domestic Korean politics and events than would otherwise be easily available, except when there's a 'surge' because of a pending missile test or nuke rumor. OSC captures a fair amount of coverage from Japanese and Chinese media, enabling more of a composite picture for U.S. government readers." This same respondent included a very detailed, surprisingly frank discussion of why and how the Chinese government was seriously displeased with North Korea for defying public warnings on the July 5, 2006, missile tests. U.S. specialists now see the points raised in that discussion as evidence of an evolving Chinese policy toward North Korea.

A former high-ranking State Department official also commented on the OSC, calling it "the single most useful source in terms of agglomerating reporting from non-American sources, not just South Korean, but also North Korean, Chinese, etc. But if is there is a breaking news story, I may expand my search to include the wire services, usually Reuters. Korean press accounts are usually pretty reliable when they use actual quotes."

Many current and former officials receive, at their request, the comprehensive daily listserv distributed by former KEI chief John Bennett. Bennett's listserv is a labor of love that he describes as follows: "I try to look at all the Korean newspaper websites (including http://dailynk.com/english) by eight in the morning [in Washington, D.C.], as the news of the day in Korea is usually posted then." Bennett then selects the mix of trade, nonproliferation, Korean domestic politics, Unification Ministry, and Blue House stories—a mix that he knows, from his own experience, will be useful for those current policymakers, advisers, and journalist/commentators who have requested his service. Former State Department official Don Keyser used to produce a similar "private service," and Keyser's often pungent comments made his creation a combination of blog and listserv that always engaged the Korea-, China-, and Taiwan-watching communities. Alas, his service is currently on hold.

Both government and private sector survey respondents said they frequently find useful citations on the Northeast Asia Peace and Security Network (NAPSNet), produced by the Nautilus Institute, and the Pacific Forum of CSIS in Hawaii. Those respondents directly concerned with nonproliferation said they regularly check the Nautilus Institute website for its analysis and reporting of this highly complex subject. More directly in the blogosphere, the daily postings of ArmsControlWonk.com keep everyone amused and on their toes. North Korea, Iran, India, and Pakistan all receive extensive coverage on this website.

Finally, it is abundantly possible to design your own listserv via the all-encompassing Google. A couple of years ago, we at *The Nelson Report* tasked Google with the simple headline "North Korea missiles," which continues to yield interesting and abundant results. A DOD staffer has chosen "North Korean missile tests" as his search term, and he notes that "it yields all sorts of goodies, much of them having little to do with missiles. It's like reading your own personal newspaper—you never quite know what you might find!" He then forwarded a particularly interesting Chinese analysis of the political impact of the recent North Korean missile test.

The final survey question asked respondents to consider whether media coverage of the Koreas displays a useful balance of political, diplomatic, and nonproliferation topics, or focuses too much on just one issue. Clearly, we front-loaded this question, based on our own experience, and the answers we received were nearly all expressed in similar terms. One frustrated DOD analyst summed up most respondents' feelings on the subject:

> ROK sources provide interesting insight into how U.S. government actions are viewed, but not at all into actual U.S. government motivations, or even necessarily U.S. government positions, although whether that's the fault of U.S. government or ROK interpretation I leave to you to decide. All tend to be shockingly bad at synthesis. We know that U.S. politics is a mélange of political, economic, diplomatic, etc. Yet "foreign" coverage in the U.S. press is generally econ news in the business section, political/ diplomatic news in the "main news" section. And on Korea overall? U.S. media coverage is usually triggered by whatever the latest Pyongyang event was or might be. Otherwise, U.S. coverage of Korea tends to fall off the face of the earth, especially compared with China coverage, and even [coverage of] Japan.

A former State Department official confirms this view. By checking listservs, the OSC, and other outlets, the official notes, "I get a reasonably rounded picture. The Korean press does tend to focus on anything 'hot,' as do media in all countries. But that's OK from my perspective, since the Koreans often have nuggets that are not repeated in other media. For example, some focus on DPRK military issues, others on ROK domestic politics, some on economics. There is much repetition, but one can get through that pretty quickly. Thus, putting them all together usually leads to a fairly complete picture."

To summarize, our conversations with fellow Korea watchers and active players in various branches of the U.S. government clearly show that there is vast room for improvement in the individual performance of both U.S. and Korean news editors and reporters. That being said, for those who have the time and energy, it is entirely possible to get a good handle on most of what is happening in South Korea and what it all might mean. Our survey respondents agreed that the same was possible, though to a much more limited extent, for events in North Korea. But even then, when one includes the increasing frankness of Chinese authorities, the resources available should help improve coverage by the more enterprising U.S. reporters. In the end, however much the information efforts of the U.S. and Korean governments might improve, such advances can only help reporters and analysts on both sides of the Pacific in the crucial task of better understanding one another's issues.

Notes

[1] In fall 2006 for *The Nelson Report*, I conducted a survey of several dozen U.S. policymakers and administration officials, officials on Capitol

Hill, think tank scholars, and journalists about the formulation of U.S. policy toward North Korea.

2 *The Nelson Report* is a subscription-only daily briefing on international economic policy issues and on foreign and security policy matters used by government and private-sector clients in the United States and Asia.

Note: Locators for figures, tables and notes are marked by "f," "t," and "n," respectively.

A

Ahn Myon-chul, 82–84
Albright, Madeleine, 30, 99, 113
al-Haideri, Adnan Ihsan Saeed, 81
anti-Americanism, anti-American protests
  contribution of news coverage to, 49–51
  diminishing of, 66, 112
  response to in U.S., 100, 130
  in South Korea, xiii, xiv, xvi, 59, 61–64, 130–33
  as theme in business coverage, 71–72
antigovernment protests. *See also* democratization
  in North Korea, 82, 91
  in South Korea, 44, 53, 55, 71
Arirang Games, Pyongyang, 2005, 89
ArmsControlWonk.com, 150
Asian financial crisis
  tone of coverage, 33
  volume of coverage, xii, 13t, 14, 21t, 22, 23, 26–27, 33, 36
Asian Games, 2002, 64
Associated Press
  series on No Gun Ri massacre, 63, 131–32
  wire feeds, as source of information, 6
Atta, Mohammed, 85

B

Bamford, James, 81
banking, stories about
  Banco Delta Asia (BDA), Macao, 93, 116, 143–44
  banking reforms, South Korea *vs.* Japan, 72–73
  Lone Star bank takeover, 71
BBC
  accuracy of coverage, 84
  BBC wire service, 103, 105, 146
  coverage of North Korea, 109
  live broadcast from North Korea, 103, 105
"the beach," Yonsei University, Seoul, 44, 58, 81
Beijing, China
  competition with news from, 45
  coverage of Korea from, xvii, 48–49, 146
  coverage of U.S. from, 147
Bennett, John, listserv, 150
Blue House (South Korea)
  accuracy of news reports about U.S. from, 149
  announcement from, as source of information, 120
Bolton, John, 141
Boucher, Richard, 114
broadcast journalism
  financial constraints, 85
  hot-spot coverage, 46, 63
  special challenges of in North Korea, 104–7
budget cuts, financial constraints, xvi, xvii, 67, 73, 83, 85
Bush, George W., Bush administration. *See also* U.S.–North Korean relations; U.S.–South Korean relations
  focus on Iraq and Iran, 87–88, 114–15, 121–23
  impact on tone of U.S. coverage of North Korea, 29, 46, 63–64, 104
  internal debates about North Korea, 113–14, 141
  news leaks, 123–24
  relationship with media and reporters, 142
  response to North Korean nuclear

and changes in coverage over
time, 22–23, 22f
defined, 5
relationship to article tone, 20–21,
21t
news coverage, 49–50. *See also*
hot-shot journalism *and specific
countries and issues*
accuracy of, 124–25, 142
analyzing, study approach, 5–6
barriers to providing context or
depth, xvi, 62, 64–66, 97–100,
104–7, 112–13, 116–17, 149
bilateral *vs.* nationalist
perspective, 23, 51–54, 70, 101,
129, 132, 133–34
competition for attention, 8, 83
current *vs.* past approaches, 48
feature stories *vs.* breaking news,
107
financial factors, 48–49, 73, 85
as form of public diplomacy,
49–50, 70, 87, 129
importance of, during periods of
crisis, 111–12, 123
influence of personal judgment,
72–73, 142–43
of Japan during the 1980s, 137
of Korean Peninsula, critiques of,
146
in North Korean newspapers, 105
relationship to U.S. policy goals,
54, 120, 142–43
role of editors in deciding what to
cover, 66
stereotyping of Koreans, 49, 62–
63, 92–93, 97, 101, 117
news focus
changes over time, 23–26, 55–56
and coverage levels, 7–8
North Korean perspective, 89–90
specific focuses, 10–12, 11t, 13t
tone and, 12–15, 14t
news sources. *See* sources of
information
Nihon Keizai Shimbun, 70
9/11 terrorist attacks, impact on
news coverage, 85–86

1994 Agreed Framework, 112,
114–15, 143
No Gun Ri massacre, 1950, 131
North Hamgyong Province, North
Korea, 91–92
North Korea. *See also*
North Korea (DPRK, Democratic
People's Republic of Korea). *See
also* Kim Jong-il; U.S.–North
Korean relations
accessibility to foreign reporters,
8, 21, 79, 87–90, 105, 111
accuracy of news about, 82–85, 149
coverage of, inter-newspaper
differences, 12, 13t
coverage of *vs.* coverage of U.S.-
Korean relations, 34
disinterest about, in U.S. press,
20–21, 83, 120
EU mission to, 2001, 103–4
feature stories about, 93–94, 100,
107
focus of articles about, changes
over time, 8, 10–12, 11t, 13t,
23–26, 55–56, 92–93
hot-spot approach to coverage of,
7–8, 45–46, 116
importance of continuing foreign
coverage, 86–87, 94–95, 123
Juche ideology, 97–98
labeling of as evil, 63–64, 98
life outside Pyongyang, 91, 107–9
negative *vs.* positive evaluations
of, 14
relations with South Korea, 63,
103, 132
sources of information about,
79–85, 89, 142, 147
tone of articles about, 18–21, 19t,
29–30
understanding perspective,
historical context, 90, 97–99,
100–102, 106, 112–13, 124
"vox pop" interviews, 105–6
North Korean Human Rights Act of
2004, 10
North Korean Workers' Party, 105
Northeast Asia Peace and Security

ABOUT THE CONTRIBUTORS

Kristin C. Burke is currently on loan from the Walter H. Shorenstein Asia-Pacific Research Center (Shorenstein APARC) to the Office of the Secretary of Defense–Policy, where she serves as country director for Korea with responsibilities for both DRPK and U.S.-ROK alliance issues. Previously, she was a research associate at Shorenstein APARC, where she developed journal articles and book chapters for the American and Korean media project, which examines U.S. and ROK media coverage of the alliance, North Korea, and inter-Korean relations. Burke was formerly an associate at AALC, limited company (formerly Armitage Associates), where she conducted ongoing analysis of East Asian political and defense issues. She earned a B.A. with University Distinction in international relations in 2001 and an M.A. in political sociology in 2002, both from Stanford University.

Martin Fackler has written extensively about Northeast Asia for more than a decade, including in his most recent capacity as Tokyo bureau chief for the *New York Times*. He has also been a correspondent in the region for the *Wall Street Journal*, the *Far Eastern Economic Review*, the Associated Press, and Bloomberg News. In 2005 he was part of a team of reporters awarded by the Society of Publishers in Asia for coverage of the Indian Ocean tsunami, and in 2008 he was part of a team of reporters nominated for the Pulitzer Prize for coverage of the global financial crisis.

Anna Fifield is the Middle East correspondent for the *Financial Times*, covering Iran, Iraq, Syria and Lebanon. Previously—from 2004 to 2008, the period during which Pyongyang conducted its first nuclear test—she served as the *Financial Times* correspondent in Seoul, covering both North and South Korea. She visited North Korea more than ten times and won a Society of Publishers in Asia award for excellence in human rights reporting for her coverage of North Korea (2008).

Caroline Gluck is a former BBC Seoul correspondent. She has spent more than a decade reporting from Asia for BBC radio, television, and online outlets. She has also reported for National Public Radio; KQED's former weekly current affairs program, "Pacific Time;" and Canada's national public broadcaster, CBC. She has been a regular contributor to publications including *The Times* (London) and *The Economist*. She currently works as globe-roving humanitarian press officer for the international aid organization Oxfam.

Donald A. L. Macintyre is currently writing a book on how the spread of markets and information is changing the lives of ordinary North Koreans. As a 2006–2007

Pantech Fellow at Shorenstein APARC, he conducted research on North Korea's economy and organized a conference on U.S. coverage of the Korean Peninsula. The chapters contained in this volume were first presented at that conference at Stanford University in July 2007.

Macintyre was head of communications at Shinsei Bank in Tokyo until March 2009. He ran *Time* magazine's Seoul bureau from 2001 to 2006, covering the nuclear crisis, general news, and the economies of North and South Korea. He has traveled to North Korea six times and made numerous trips to China's border with North Korea to interview defectors, refugees, and traders. During 2006 he served as a senior adviser to the International Crisis Group on the North Korea refugee issue.

Before setting up *Time*'s first permanent bureau in Seoul in 2001, Macintyre was a correspondent for *Time* in Tokyo. Previously, he worked for Bloomberg News as a reporter, editor, and feature writer. He has also reported for *AsiaWeek*, Canada's CBC Radio, and Vatican Radio.

The New York State Society of Certified Public Accountants awarded Macintyre its Excellence in Financial Journalism Award in 1997 for an investigative article on price manipulation in Japanese stock markets. He received the Overseas Press Club of America's Honorable Mention in the category of "Best Newspaper or News Service Reporting from Abroad" for the same story.

B. R. Myers was born in New Jersey and raised in Bermuda, South Africa, and Germany. He has a Ph.D. in North Korean Studies from the University of Tubingen, Germany. His books include *Han Sorya and North Korean Literature* (1994) and *A Reader's Manifesto* (2002). At present he is the director of the international studies department at Dongseo University in Busan, South Korea. In addition to writing literary criticism for *The Atlantic*, of which he is a contributing editor, Myers regularly contributes articles on North Korea to the *New York Times*, the *Wall Street Journal*, and academic journals. His next book, an analysis of the North Korean worldview, will be published in early 2010.

Chris Nelson is a senior vice president of Samuels International Associates, a Washington, D.C. consulting firm where he serves as editor and publisher of *The Nelson Report*, a daily "insider's" look at foreign policy and trade issues.

Nelson has been a consultant since leaving Capitol Hill in 1983, when he joined Teramura International, a new company designed to facilitate U.S.-Japan business and diplomatic relations. What became *The Nelson Report* started at that time. Nelson joined Samuels International in 1997. *The Nelson Report* is an interactive information service that uses e-mail, phone, and fax to allow clients both to pose private questions for their own use and to seek details from the daily report.

Nelson has spent his professional life as a journalist and Asia policy specialist with a focus on Japan, China, and Korea. He began his career in 1967 with United Press International, in New York, and has also worked extensively on

Capitol Hill with notable roles on the Senate Democratic Policy Committee and the House International Relations Subcommittee on Asia, where he handled normalization of U.S. relations with China. He currently travels and lectures in China, Japan, South Korea, and Taiwan on a regular basis.

He has published two books and countless articles on the Civil War, is a contributing editor to *Military Images Magazine*, and has been interviewed on numerous television specials, including "Civil War Journal."

Nelson graduated from Phillips Academy, Andover, in 1962, and the University of California, Berkeley, in 1967. He completed graduate studies at McGill University, Montreal, in 1970.

David E. Sanger is the chief Washington correspondent for the *New York Times*. A 1982 graduate of Harvard College, Sanger has been writing for the *Times* for over twenty-six years, covering foreign policy, globalization, nuclear proliferation, and the presidency. He has been a member of two teams that won the Pulitzer Prize, and has been awarded numerous honors for national security and foreign policy coverage. His first book, *The Inheritance: The World Obama Confronts and the Challenges to American Power* (2009), was a bestseller.

Before coming to Washington in 1994, Sanger was a correspondent and then chief of the *Times'* Tokyo bureau. There, he developed a specialization in writing on the influence of economics and foreign policy, and the relationships between the United States and its major allies, a subject he continues to pursue in Washington. He also wrote many of the first articles about North Korea's nuclear weapons program. Sanger left Asia in 1994 to become the chief Washington economic correspondent. Later, he was named a senior writer and White House correspondent. He was with President Bush on 9/11 and covered two wars, Iraq and Afghanistan. He also played a central role in the first stories that uncovered the nuclear proliferation ring run by Abdul Qadeer Khan, the Pakistani metallurgist who helped sell technology to Iran, North Korea, and Libya. That investigation became the core of "Nuclear Jihad: Can Terrorists Get the Bomb?" which won the Columbia/DuPont Award in 2007.

As a newcomer to the *Times*, Sanger was a member of the team that won the Pulitzer for national reporting on its investigation of the space agency following the Challenger disaster. Later, he was among another Pulitzer-winning team to write about the Clinton administration's struggle to control exports to China. In 2004 he and four other colleagues also shared the American Society of Newspaper Editors' top award for deadline writing for their team coverage of the Columbia disaster. He has also won the Weintal Prize for Diplomatic Reporting, for coverage of the Korean and Iraq crises in 2003, and several awards from the White House Correspondents' Association.

Karl Schoenberger has written about politics, culture, and economic development in Asia throughout his twenty-five years in journalism, working as a foreign correspondent in Tokyo for the *Los Angeles Times*, the *Asian Wall Street Journal*, and the Associated Press, and in Hong Kong for *Fortune* magazine.

Now based in San Francisco, Schoenberger is currently a research fellow at the Human Rights Center at the University of California, Berkeley. He is also finishing his first novel. His most recent stint as a journalist was at the *San Jose Mercury News*, where he worked as a business editor, reporter, and Pacific Rim correspondent. During a hiatus from the *Mercury News*, he wrote about the cultural dimensions of the Internet economy as a contributing writer for *The Industry Standard* and published articles in the *New York Times* and other publications.

In 2003, Schoenberger received the Overseas Press Club's Whitman Bassow Award for Environmental Reporting for his work at the *Mercury News* on electronic waste dumping in China. Schoenberger has also served as a teaching fellow at the Graduate School of Journalism at the University of California, Berkeley, where he wrote the book *Levi's Children: Coming to Terms with Human Rights in the Global Marketplace* (2001).

He received his bachelor's degree in Japanese language and literature from Stanford University and did graduate work in communications at Stanford. He has studied at Kyoto University as a Monbusho Scholar and at Harvard University as a Nieman Fellow.

Gi-Wook Shin is the director of Shorenstein APARC; the Tong Yang, Korea Foundation, and Korea Stanford Alumni Chair of Korean Studies; the founding director of the Korean Studies Program; senior fellow at the Freeman Spogli Institute for International Studies; and professor of sociology at Stanford University. As a historical-comparative and political sociologist, his research has concentrated on areas of social movements, nationalism, development, and international relations. Shin has served as editor of the *Journal of Korean Studies*, a premier journal in the field of Korean studies.

Shin is the author/editor of many books and articles, including: *Cross-Currents: Regionalism and Nationalism in Northeast Asia* (2007); *Rethinking Historical Injustice and Reconciliation in Northeast Asia* (2006); *Ethnic Nationalism in Korea: Genealogy, Politics and Legacy* (2006); *North Korea: 2005 and Beyond* (2006); *Contentious Kwangju* (2004); *Colonial Modernity in Korea* (1999); and *Peasant Protest and Social Change in Colonial Korea* (1996). His articles have appeared in academic journals, such as the *American Journal of Sociology, Nations and Nationalism, Comparative Studies in Society and History, International Sociology, Asian Survey*, and *Asian Perspectives*.

Shin has just completed a new book titled *One Alliance, Two Lenses: U.S.-Korea Relations in a New Era* (Stanford University Press, 2009). It is based on analyses of more than 8,000 newspaper articles published in the U.S. and South Korean media from 1992 to 2004. He is editing two more books with his colleagues, respectively titled *Divided Memories and Reconciliation in Northeast Asia* and *From Democracy to Civil Society in Korea*. He is also engaged in a project addressing historical injustice and reconciliation in Northeast Asia with a particular focus on the U.S. responsibility and role in resolving the history question in that region.

Shin is not only the recipient of numerous grants and fellowships but has also actively raised funds for Korean/Asian studies at Stanford. He gives frequent lectures and seminars on topics ranging from Korean nationalism and politics to Korea's foreign relations and the plight and history of Korean Americans. He also writes op-eds in Korean and American newspapers and serves on councils and advisory boards in the United States and South Korea.

Before coming to Stanford, Shin taught at the University of Iowa and the University of California, Los Angeles. After receiving his B.A. from Yonsei University in Korea, he was awarded his M.A. and Ph.D. from the University of Washington.

Barbara Slavin is assistant managing editor for world and national security of the *Washington Times* and the author of a book on Iran titled *Bitter Friends, Bosom Enemies: Iran, the U.S. and the Twisted Path to Confrontation* (2007).

Before joining the *Times* in July 2008, she was senior diplomatic reporter for *USA Today*, responsible for analyzing foreign news and U.S. foreign policy. Beginning in 1996, she covered such key issues as the U.S.-led war on terrorism and in Iraq, policy toward "rogue" states, and the Arab-Israeli conflict. She accompanied three secretaries of state on their official travels and also reported from Iran, Libya, Israel, Egypt, North Korea, Russia, China, Saudi Arabia, and Syria. Slavin—who has lived in Russia, China, Japan, and Egypt—is a regular commentator on U.S. foreign policy on National Public Radio, the Public Broadcasting System, and C-Span. She wrote her book on Iran, which she has visited seven times, as a public policy scholar at the Woodrow Wilson International Center for Scholars in 2006 and spent October 2007–July 2008 as senior fellow at the U.S. Institute of Peace, where she researched and wrote a report on Iranian regional influence, titled "Mullahs, Money and Militias: How Iran Exerts Its Influence in the Middle East."

Prior to joining *USA Today*, she was a Washington-based writer for *The Economist* and the *Los Angeles Times*, covering domestic and foreign policy issues, including the 1991–1993 Middle East peace talks in Washington. From 1985–1989, she was *The Economist* correspondent in Cairo. She traveled widely in the Middle East, covering the Iran-Iraq war, the 1986 U.S. bombing of Libya, the political evolution of the Palestine Liberation Organization, and the resurgence of Islamic fundamentalism. Earlier in the 1980s, she served as *The Economist* correspondent in Beijing and also reported from Japan and South Korea. Prior to moving abroad, she was a writer and editor for the *New York Times* Week in Review section and a reporter and editor for United Press International in New York City.

Slavin earned her B.A. in Russian language and literature at Harvard University and also studied at Leningrad State University. She is a member of the Council on Foreign Relations.

171

Daniel C. Sneider is the associate director for research at the Walter H. Shorenstein Asia-Pacific Research Center at Stanford University. He currently directs the center's project on nationalism and regionalism and the Divided Memories and Reconciliation project, a three-year comparative study of the formation of historical memory in East Asia. His own research is focused on current U.S. foreign and national security policy in Asia, including work on a diplomatic history of the building of the United States' Cold War alliances in Northeast Asia.

Sneider was a longtime foreign correspondent and most recently the foreign affairs columnist of the *San Jose Mercury News*. His twice-weekly column looking at international issues and national security from a West Coast perspective was syndicated nationally on the Knight Ridder Tribune wire service. Previously, Sneider served as national/foreign editor of the *San Jose Mercury News*. From 1990 to1994, he was the Moscow Bureau chief of the *Christian Science Monitor*, covering the end of Soviet Communism and the collapse of the Soviet Union. From 1985 to1990, he was Tokyo correspondent for the *Monitor*, covering Japan and Korea. Prior to that he was a correspondent in India, covering South and Southeast Asia. He also wrote widely on defense issues, including as a contributor and correspondent for *Defense News*, the national defense weekly.

Sneider's writings have appeared in many publications, including the *Washington Post*, the *New York Times*, the *New Republic*, *National Review*, the *Far Eastern Economic Review*, the *Oriental Economist*, *Newsweek*, *Time*, the *International Herald Tribune*, the *Financial Times*, and *Yale Global*. He is the coeditor of *Cross Currents: Regionalism and Nationalism in Northeast Asia* (Shorenstein APARC, 2007), as well as a forthcoming volume on regionalism in South Asia. He has also contributed to other volumes, including "Strategic Abandonment: Alliance Relations in Northeast Asia in the Post-Iraq Era" in *Towards Sustainable Economic and Security Relations in East Asia: U.S. and ROK Policy Options* (2008).

Sneider has a B.A. from Columbia University in East Asian history and a master's in public administration from the John F. Kennedy School of Government at Harvard University.

David Straub was named associate director of the Korean Studies Program at the Walter H. Shorenstein Asia-Pacific Research Center in 2008. Previously he was a 2007–2008 Pantech Fellow at the center. Straub is currently writing a book on recent U.S.–South Korean relations. He is also a member of the New Beginnings policy research group on U.S.–South Korean relations, which is cosponsored by Shorenstein APARC and the New York-based Korea Society.

An educator and commentator on current Northeast Asian affairs, Straub retired from the U.S. Department of State in 2006 as a senior foreign service officer after a thirty-year career focused on Northeast Asian affairs. He worked for over twelve years on Korean affairs, first arriving in Seoul in 1979, just months before the assassination of President Park Chung-hee.

Straub served as head of the political section at the U.S. embassy in Seoul from 1999 to 2002 during popular protests against the United States. He played a key working-level role in the Six-Party Talks on North Korea's nuclear program as the State Department's Korea country desk director from 2002 to 2004. He also served eight years at the U.S. embassy in Japan. His final assignment was as the State Department's Japan country desk director from 2004 to 2006, when he was coleader of the U.S. delegation to talks with Japan on the realignment of the U.S.-Japan alliance and of U.S. military bases in Japan.

After leaving the Department of State, Straub taught U.S.-Korean relations at the Johns Hopkins University's School of Advanced International Studies (SAIS) and at the Graduate School of International Studies (GSIS) of Seoul National University. He has published a number of papers on U.S.–Korean relations.

Doug Struck covered the Koreas for the *Washington Post* as Northeast Asian Bureau chief from 1999 to 2003. During that time, he reported from North Korea twice and did extensive reporting throughout South Korea with colleague Joohee Cho.

Struck has been a journalist for nearly thirty-five years, covering a wide range of assignments as both a national and foreign correspondent for the *Washington Post* and the *Baltimore Sun*. In his career, Struck reported from all fifty of the United States and six continents.

His reporting included more than a dozen assignments to Iraq over fourteen years. He helped cover conflicts in Iraq, Afghanistan, the West Bank, Lebanon, East Timor, the southern Philippines, and Sudan. He was a bureau chief based in the Middle East from the first Gulf War in 1991 to 1996, in Tokyo from 1999 to 2003, and in Toronto from 2004 to 2007.

Struck was a Nieman Fellow at Harvard University from 2003 to 2004, a Pulitzer Prize finalist in 2002, and a fellow in Asian Studies at George Washington University from 1998 to 1999. He wrote at the Harvard University Center for the Environment and has taught at Boston University. He now teaches at Emerson College as a journalist in residence. He writes and freelances extensively on environmental issues.

RECENT AND FORTHCOMING PUBLICATIONS OF THE WALTER H. SHORENSTEIN ASIA-PACIFIC RESEARCH CENTER

Books (distributed by the Brookings Institution Press)

Rafiq Dossani, Daniel C. Sneider, and Vikram Sood. *Does South Asia Exist? Prospects for Regional Integration in South Asia.* Stanford, CA: Walter H. Shorenstein Asia-Pacific Research Center, forthcoming 2009.

Jean C. Oi, Scott Rozelle, and Xueguang Zhou. *Growing Pains: Tensions and Opportunities in China's Transformation.* Stanford, CA: Walter H. Shorenstein Asia-Pacific Research Center, forthcoming 2009.

Karen Eggleston, ed. *Prescribing Cultures and Pharmaceutical Policy in the Asia-Pacific.* Stanford, CA: Walter H. Shorenstein Asia-Pacific Research Center, 2009.

Steven Reed, Kenneth Mori McElwain, and Kay Shimizu, eds. *Political Change in Japan: Electoral Behavior, Party Realignment, and the Koizumi Reforms.* Stanford, CA: Walter H. Shorenstein Asia-Pacific Research Center, 2009.

Donald K. Emmerson. *Hard Choices: Security, Democracy, and Regionalism in Southeast Asia.* Stanford, CA: Walter H. Shorenstein Asia-Pacific Research Center, 2008.

Henry S. Rowen, Marguerite Gong Hancock, and William F. Miller, eds. *Greater China's Quest for Innovation.* Stanford, CA: Walter H. Shorenstein Asia-Pacific Research Center, 2008.

Gi-Wook Shin and Daniel C. Sneider, eds. *Cross Currents: Regionalism and Nationalism in Northeast Asia.* Stanford, CA: Walter H. Shorenstein Asia-Pacific Research Center, 2007.

Stella R. Quah, ed. *Crisis Preparedness: Asia and the Global Governance of Epidemics.* Stanford, CA: Walter H. Shorenstein Asia-Pacific Research Center, 2007.

Philip W. Yun and Gi-Wook Shin, eds. *North Korea: 2005 and Beyond*. Stanford, CA:Walter H. Shorenstein Asia-Pacific Research Center, 2006.

Jongryn Mo and Daniel I. Okimoto, eds. *From Crisis to Opportunity: Financial Globalization and East Asian Capitalism*. Stanford, CA: Walter H. Shorenstein Asia-Pacific Research Center, 2006.

Michael H. Armacost and Daniel I. Okimoto, eds. *The Future of America's Alliances in Northeast Asia*. Stanford, CA: Walter H. Shorenstein Asia-Pacific Research Center, 2004.

Henry S. Rowen and Sangmok Suh, eds. *To the Brink of Peace: New Challenges in Inter-Korean Economic Cooperation and Integration*. Stanford, CA: Walter H. Shorenstein Asia-Pacific Research Center, 2001.

Studies of the Walter H. Shorenstein Asia-Pacific Research Center
(published with Stanford University Press)

Jean Oi and Nara Dillon, eds. *At the Crossroads of Empires: Middlemen, Social Networks, and State-building in Republican Shanghai*. Stanford, CA: Stanford University Press, 2007.

Henry S. Rowen, Marguerite Gong Hancock, and William F. Miller, eds. *Making IT: The Rise of Asia in High Tech*. Stanford, CA: Stanford University Press, 2006.

Gi-Wook Shin. *Ethnic Nationalism in Korea: Genealogy, Politics, and Legacy*. Stanford, CA:Stanford University Press, 2006.

Andrew Walder, Joseph Esherick, and Paul Pickowicz, eds. *The Chinese Cultural Revolution as History*. Stanford, CA: Stanford University Press, 2006.

Rafiq Dossani and Henry S. Rowen, eds. *Prospects for Peace in South Asia*. Stanford, CA: Stanford University Press, 2005.

The authorized representative in the EU for product safety and compliance is:
Mare Nostrum Group
B.V Doelen 72
4831 GR Breda
The Netherlands

www.ingramcontent.com/pod-product-compliance
Lightning Source LLC
Chambersburg PA
CBHW020354270326
41926CB00007B/426

* 9 7 8 1 9 3 1 3 6 8 1 5 5 *